HIGHLY VISIBLE
MARKETING

HIGHLY VISIBLE
MARKETING

115 LOW-COST WAYS TO AVOID
MARKET OBSCURITY

DALE R. SCHMELTZLE, CPA

DEDICATION

Dale Carnegie was a bestselling American writer and lecturer. He is perhaps best known as the author of *How to Win Friends and Influence People,* which remains popular more than half a century after his death. One of his most famous quotes was, "When life hands you lemons, make lemonade!"

This book is dedicated to a new groundswell of hard-working men and women who, through no fault of their own, were forced to become entrepreneurs when the economic conditions of recent years displaced them from their previously comfortable and seemingly predictable lives in corporate America. You are factory workers, contractors, engineers, sales people, artisans, computer technicians, welders and public servants, just to name a few.

You are not marketing specialists or accountants. Yet to be successful as a new small business owner you must possess this essential knowledge, or have access to someone who does.

I wrote this book to provide that access and to help you succeed in your new venture. If just one small business finds a single idea within these pages that allows them to grow and prosper, I will have accomplished my goal.

Let's make some lemonade!

Contents

FOREWORD

The title and subject of this book IS *HIGHLY VISIBLE* MARKETING - 115 LOW-COST WAYS TO AVOID MARKET OBSCURITY. Therefore, let me first say that if you are a marketing expert, or if you can afford to hire one, then this book is not for you. It was written specifically for small businesses, those lacking both personal marketing experience and a staff with adequate resources to support a dedicated marketing function.

Obscurity means existing in a state of darkness, anonymity or insignificance. **I refuse to believe that any business venture is predestined to obscurity.** Rather, obscurity is an insidious enemy, often ensnaring us in its inescapable stranglehold before we realize we were in danger of falling victim to it. It may be the ultimate result of a series of bad business decisions, or too often merely the failure to act decisively at key junctures. Whatever the cause, market obscurity in a competitive business environment is usually a precursor to failure, or at best mediocrity. It is certainly incompatible with success. **By definition, a business that achieves "highly visible marketing" cannot be obscure.**

Let me relate the story of one entrepreneur who had to overcome many obstacles to avoid obscurity in his personal and business life.

Will Keith (W.K.) Kellogg was born shortly before the Civil War, the nearsighted and painfully shy son of pioneer parents. Labeled "dimwitted" by his teachers, he quit school at 14 to become a broom salesman. He held that job for 6 years. W.K. then worked as a bookkeeper and business manager at the Battle Creek Sanitarium, a church-affiliated health resort where his older brother John was superintendent. He labored there for 26 years, often working 120-hour weeks. Many of those hours were spent searching for a digestible substitute for bread. His experimentation was often conducted in plain view of Sanitarium guests, including C.W. Post.

Finally, at the age of 46, his efforts resulted in the invention of corn flakes. He was eventually forced to part ways with John, who saw no market potential for breakfast cereals. W.K. founded the Kellogg Company in 1906, eleven years after Post Cereals was founded. In July of the following year, the Kellogg plant burned to the ground. Always known as a man who believed in hard work instead of fate, W.K. rebuilt a fireproof plant from its ashes.

Although he had every excuse to live a quiet life in complete obscurity, W.K. Kellogg founded what is today the world's largest producer of breakfast cereals. Over 30,000 employees can testify that his legacy is not one of obscurity, by any definition of the word.

Corporate history is replete with people like W.K. Kellogg. Countless small businesses started in garages, basements, railroad stations and similar humble origins went on to become extraordinarily successful. The list includes Ford, Kodak and Sears just to name few. All had at least one thing in common. They all had to avoid the trap of market obscurity and pull ahead of their competition. To accomplish that, they had to deliver a superior product or service. They also had to differentiate their brand and communicate its benefits to potential customers.

Where will the next Ford, Kodak or Sears come from? For that matter, is that level of success even achievable in today's challenging economic environment? After all, Henry Ford, George Eastman and Richard Warren Sears did not have to worry about global competition or the latest Internet marketing platform. They simply marketed their brands' unique advantages on pieces of paper in the form of catalogs, magazines, and newspapers.

While we cannot predict the future, there is one thing we can say with complete certainty. The pool of potential Fortune 500 companies is huge. U.S. Census Bureau statistics (as compiled by the 2007 County Business Patterns and 2007 Economic Census) show that non-farm employers with fewer than 100 workers employed 42.7 million people, over 35% of the entire civilian labor force. Those employers represented over 80% of all businesses. They had total estimated annual revenues of $7.8 trillion. The Census Bureau also reported that the 5.7 million businesses with revenue under $5 million encompassed 94% of all American firms.

There is no question that small businesses comprise a huge and vital part of our national economy, no matter how you define the term. I am a small businessperson.

I am also a CPA, someone who understands how numbers predict, measure and ultimately determine success or failure. **I understand that growing a business and increasing profits are not automatically synonymous.** I also understand statistics such as this one: 35% of small businesses do not survive to celebrate their first anniversary. Fewer than 15% will see their fifth anniversary.

That is precisely why I have written this marketing book from a financial perspective, to empower you with practical and cost effective ways to increase sales without inadvertently sabotaging your "bottom line." My goal is to help you beat the odds. It is, quite simply, to help you overcome the market obscurity that eventually ensnares the majority of new ventures.

Before I present a list of ways to grow your business and increase profits, it is essential to establish a context and a framework for their successful evaluation and implementation in your business. The list will follow, beginning in Chapter 2.

Chapter 1

KNOWLEDGE IS POWER

Sixteenth century English philosopher Sir Francis Bacon is credited with first saying, "Knowledge is power." Actually, the closest phrase historians can find in his writings is, "Human knowledge and human power meet in one; for where  the cause is not known the effect cannot be produced."

Regardless of who said it, the statement is never truer than when making business decisions in a dynamic and highly competitive environment. "Knowing your numbers" requires that every businessperson possess a clear understanding of two things in order to establish a marketing budget and implement successful marketing campaigns: the specific goals to be accomplished; and, the financial consequences of changes in customer behavior on sales, gross profit and net income.

It has been said that the goal of marketing is to persuade consumers of three things:

A. They need to buy your product or service;

B. They need to buy your product or service from you; and

C. They need to buy your product or service from you right now!

In other words, the purpose of marketing is to influence consumer behavior in ways that accomplish your business goals. What exactly do you want to accomplish? Do you want to stimulate sales during a post-holiday slump; clear out seasonal, overstocked or discontinued merchandise; introduce a new product line; sell specific high-margin products; or just get more people through your front door? Each of those objectives requires its own set of tactics.

Begin your planning process by making a list of your marketing and business goals. They should be consistent with your value proposition (see Appendix I) and business philosophy. **Include financial and non-monetary objectives, along with realistic timeframes for each goal. Try to be as specific as possible.** A goal of simply increasing sales is neither constructive nor measurable. A goal of increasing sales 5% per month for the next six months through a combination of a 4% increase in customer count and a $17 increase in average dollars per sale is. If your timeframe extends over a long period, say a year or more, you will also need to establish interim benchmarks to measure short-term progress toward your ultimate goals. That will allow you to take timely corrective action or readjust your goals as needed.

After you have defined your goals, structure promotions to ensure accountability toward their accomplishment. Be able to measure incremental sales and to segregate the results of simultaneous promotions. Compare results against expectations and the cost of the promotion. **Accountability is a paramount management concept that underlies every suggestion in this book.**

Accountability Questions:

Here is a sample of the types of accountability questions you should be able to answer, both before and after a promotion. Inherent in each question is the assumption that you have an accounting system capable of capturing and reporting the supporting data. Additionally, the last two questions may require a count of people entering your store or contacting your office.

You can undoubtedly add to the list. I encourage you to tailor it to your specific business and circumstances. If available, compare your numbers to industry norms and analyze significant variances.

A. What is your gross profit (sales price less the cost of goods sold) on every item in your inventory?

B. What are your inventory turnover rates by major category? Inventory turnover is defined as the cost of sales divided by average inventory value. For example, if your annual cost of sales is $1.2 million and your average inventory (at cost) is $218 thousand, your turnover rate is 5.5. That means on average every item in your inventory is sold and restocked 5.5 times per year. Generally, the higher the ratio, the more efficiently you are utilizing your invested capital. However, at some point a high turnover may indicate the potential loss of sales if items are out of stock too frequently.

C. What are your average sales by day of the week and month?

D. What is your average dollar sale per transaction?

E. What percentage of sales is from new customers versus repeat customers?

F. Who are your most profitable and least profitable customers; what characteristics distinguish one category from the other?

G. What percentage of sales (by meaningful categories) is returned?

H. What is your average customer retention? Customer retention means how long your customers continue to do business with you.

I. What is your average customer traffic (or sales transactions) by day and within meaningful time frames (morning versus afternoon, etc.)?

J. What is your closing ratio, or the percentage of prospects that actually make a purchase?

You have several alternatives to measuring traffic and closing rates. The simplest (and most expensive) is to install electronic sensors on doors. This works well for most high-volume retail businesses, especially if customers enter and exit through one door, and employees use another. If everyone uses one entrance, sensors can be programmed to start counting only when the store opens, or with the first recorded sale of the day. For lower volume establishments, you might consider keeping manual counts or just track the number of bid requests or proposals. Finally, you can simply monitor the number of sales transactions and study changes over time.

None of these methods are perfect. For example, electronic sensors count everyone twice (entering and leaving). They also include accompanying children and others who cannot realistically be considered prospects. However, as long as the counting methodology is used consistently, it will begin to disclose meaningful trends and allow you to monitor changes in traffic because of your marketing efforts.

Knowing things like who responded to your promotion (repeat vs. new customers), what they did (bought only sale items or made additional purchases) and when they did it (for example, traditionally slow mid-week traffic increased 14%) are important in your accountability analysis and evaluation.

If the costs of your promotion exceed the ultimate benefits, take a page out of Thomas Edison's playbook. When challenged about experimenting with over 10,000 different substances before picking a carbon filament for his light bulb, he replied, "I have not failed. I've just found 10,000 ways that won't work." Learning that something won't work is valuable information. **If a new marketing idea fails to generate the intended results after you have given it**

sufficient time to succeed, simply cross it off your list and move on to the next idea.

If all that sounds fairly basic, you may be in the minority. A 2005 study titled *Small Business: Causes of Bankruptcy* by Don B. Bradley III and Chris Cowdery of the University of Central Arkansas reported that of businesses in their study that filed for bankruptcy, 58% admitted to doing "little to no record keeping." I assume the actual number probably exceeded the number willing to admit it.

Regardless of the exact percentage, the fact is far too many small businesses fail to maintain adequate accounting and record keeping systems. **Do not fall into the trap of thinking your accounting system is nothing more than an unavoidable burden to placate the Internal Revenue Service.** Fully utilized, it is arguably your most important management tool. Software products as basic, inexpensive and widely supported as QuickBooks or Sage Peachtree can address the needs of most small businesses.

Without an adequate accounting system, a business cannot fully understand its revenue cycle. Nor can it know the actual cost of products and services, or measure results. For these unfortunate businesses, making informed marketing decisions is simply not possible. They are forced to react blindly from a position of weakness rather than to be able to act confidently from a position of knowledge.

Accountability Examples:

Two examples will further illustrate the importance of knowing your numbers.

Although there are valid business reasons to occasionally offer products or provide services at a loss, you cannot continually sell something for $75 that cost you $100 and expect to make up the difference on volume! Your gross profit margin sets a limit on how low you can routinely price a product or service in order to cover operating expenses and still make a profit. If your full price gross margin is 32%, a 25% promotional discount affords a small gross profit; a 50% discount does not.

Knowing your numbers can be far more challenging for manufacturers and service providers than for retailers, but is no less crucial.

Now assume your average sale is $127 at an average gross profit margin of 23%. Further, assume the average customer makes 3.8 purchases per year. Your customer is expected to generate $483 in sales and $111 in gross profit annually. If customer retention averages 4 years, they are worth a gross profit or undiscounted value of $444.

Both examples demonstrate limits that exist on all marketing efforts. High margin products and high repeat sales support high marketing budgets and discounts; low margins and low repeat sales do not.

Ask yourself right now, "Do I really know where my business fits in that continuum?" **If you regularly exceed**

your limits, marketing actions that seem perfectly reasonable could eventually lead you down an irreversible path to failure.

For a decision maker in your position, Sir Francis Bacon's statement should be restated, "knowledge is survival."

As you review the list of marketing ideas in this book, recognize not all will be appropriate for your business. Others will require significant modification to fit your needs. My goal is not to present a "one size fits all" magic formula for marketing success; that does not exist. Nor is it to provide in-depth, highly technical discussions and analysis of each idea.

My goal is to be thought provoking and to challenge and encourage you to experiment with cost effective strategies and new concepts in order to communicate your message to an ever-expanding list of customers and prospects. As you experiment, you must be able to measure and compare the costs and benefits of every promotion.

Above all, be flexible, open-minded and willing to try multiple marketing strategies at once. Remember the words of Jay Abraham, American business author and self-proclaimed marketing wizard. He said, "If you're attacking your market from multiple positions and your competition isn't, you have all the advantage and it will show up in your increased success and income."

As promised, here are my 115 LOW-COST WAYS TO AVOID MARKET OBSCURITY. I estimate approximately two-thirds of these ideas can be implemented without any out-of-pocket expenses, only the cost of your own time. Most should be less than $100, and few if any should exceed a 3-figure investment. I have also included numerous examples, quotes, tips, additional references and free resources to assist in your understanding, evaluation and successful implementation of the ideas.

Now let's get to that list!

<u>Chapter 2</u>

GROWTH THROUGH NETWORKING

The word "network" means to meet and interact with people for the purpose of making contacts, building relationships and exchanging ideas and information. That sounds simple enough. Unfortunately, this simple word is a major obstacle for many would-  be entrepreneurs. Whether you are comfortable in front of large groups and talking with strangers or not, it is imperative that you communicate your story to as many people as possible.

Ralph Waldo Emerson once said, "Build a better mousetrap and the world will beat a path to your door." I doubt Emerson's statement was true of any product without an adequate marketing plan to promote it. In all fairness, he died 109 years before the introduction of the Internet. I am quite certain it is a guaranteed formula for failure in today's fast-paced marketplace.

In other words, customers will not "beat a path to your door" unless you give them a reason to go there. You must first tell them why your mousetrap is better or cheaper than other available products. If you fail to provide an adequate level of education, you leave to chance whether potential customers will trade with you or a competitor across town, or even across the globe.

Robert G. Allen, author of several New York Times bestselling personal finance books said this, "No matter what your product is, you are ultimately in the education business. Your customers need to be constantly educated about the many advantages of doing business with you, trained to use your products more effectively, and taught how to make never-ending improvement in their lives."

Networking is a good place to begin communicating with and educating others, especially since the only out-of-pocket cost is usually a meal. Before you grit your teeth and jump into networking with both feet, a little advanced preparation will help break the ice and perhaps calm the butterflies in your stomach when meeting strangers.

Here are six quick tips to help build personal relationships through networking. They apply to every idea in this chapter.

A. If the networking event includes a meal or appetizers, avoid eating while meeting people. If it includes adult beverages, keep your alcohol consumption to a minimum.

B. Greet each new person you meet with a firm handshake. Maintain eye contact. Ask questions and learn about their business, especially how you can help them. Let them do most of the talking while you practice your active listening skills.

C. Do not trust your memory. Take notes on their business card. Review those notes before every meeting until you can remember the name and background of people you have already met. If necessary, spell their name phonetically to remember the proper pronunciation.

D. It has been said that a person's name is their favorite word. Be sure to greet contacts by name in subsequent meetings. Yahoo co-founder Jerry Yang stated an obvious corollary to this point, "It helps a ton when you learn people's names and don't butcher them when trying to pronounce them." With a name like Schmeltzle, I know where he is coming from! Moreover, someone who remembers names is often considered someone who pays attention to details, a highly desirable trait in most business settings.

E. Attitude is everything! Remember that networking is based on the concept that you first help others in order to be helped. Become recognized as the "go to" problem solver in the group and members will begin to seek you out.

F. Finally, always have plenty of business cards in your pocket, purse or briefcase. I will talk more about business cards in Idea #16.

Networking 101:

The following networking ideas will help market yourself and your business.

1. Your "10-second speech" is your initial announcement of who you are and what you do. Write it down and practice your speech in private. My speech goes something like this, "Hello. My name is Dale Schmeltzle, CPA, and my company is CFO America. We are a fractional or part-time consulting firm, and we provide finance, accounting and strategic management solutions for your business." Whatever you say, communicate your message confidently, concisely and consistently. It is very true that you only get one chance to make a good first impression.

2. A witty but simple tag line or slogan will help others remember you. I have a network contact who sells industrial gloves and safety equipment. He ends his 10-second speech with, "How's your glove life?" I have another contact whose owns a residential and commercial roofing company. He ends with, "We handle all your roofing needs, from your dog house to your warehouse." I always remember both businesses.

3. Wear a permanent nametag. I found myself engaged in a losing battle to reapply the stick-on variety. They invariably fell off during every meeting. That was a distraction I did not need when dealing with the already stressful situation of introducing myself to a room full of strangers. The problem was solved by investing $12 in a magnetically secured nametag complete with my business logo. I purchased it at Sign-A-Rama from a contact I meet through networking. If you do not have a similar local vendor, you can order a nametag online.

4. Focus on the quality of your network contacts, not the quantity. Dale Carnegie said, "You can make more friends in two months by being interested in other people than you can in two years by trying to get people interested in you." For that reason, I suggest you limit new contacts to no more than two or three at each meeting. I also suggest you consider the size of groups and avoid those that are simply too large to establish meaningful relationships with substantially all members.

5. Search the Internet for local business networks. Start with www.meetup.com, a free service that provides information on 250,000 monthly meetings in 45,000 cities. Meetup has several other features you will find useful including meeting agendas and guest speakers, reminders and member pictures and profiles. After you have "kicked a few tires" choose several groups to join, but do not spread yourself too thin. The only way to gain the full benefit of networking is to participate. Attend networking meetings as often as your schedule permits.

   • Make every effort to eventually meet all of the regular attendees and familiarize yourself with their businesses. This may be best accomplished in one-on-one or individual meetings outside of the group setting. I often meet with members over a cup of coffee.

- You may also find new vendor connections that are as valuable as new marketing opportunities, especially when first launching your business.

- Publicly thank members who provide referrals, services or advice.

6. W. C. Fields liked to joke that he would not join a club that would have him as a member. The opposite occurs in networking groups who practice exclusivity in their membership. Many allow only one person from each profession or category. Make the exclusivity issue your first question. If it applies and a local competitor beat you to the group, you may still have the option of redefining yourself for purposes of membership. For example, although you typically introduce yourself as an insurance agent, perhaps the group can allow you to be the commercial insurance agent without upsetting another agent who specializes in accident and health insurance.

7. Make sure your product or a gift certificate for your service is occasionally given as a door prize. Giving away a decorative basket of your products is an especially nice touch! You can also offer tickets to a sporting event or a charity function as a door prize. However, give a minimum of two adjoining seats and try not to hand them out on short notice. That will depreciate the value of your gift in the eyes of the recipient.

8. Consider joining trade groups and professional associations dedicated to your occupation or business.

Your initial reaction might be why waste time with people who are competing for the same customers, especially since many will be larger and more established than you are. I can offer two reasons:

- First, you will probably gain a lot of valuable information about new technology, business procedures, new products, better sub-contractors and less expensive suppliers and vendors. You may even establish mentoring relationships with more seasoned members.

- Secondly, you may find other members occasionally refer overflow work or jobs that are just too small for them. You can sometimes make a nice living off the crumbs that fall from the king's table.

9. Think about Google and Facebook for a moment. Their initial marketing strategy was to build a following or customer base by creating something of great value, and then giving it away. It may have sounded crazy, but it is hard to argue with their results. Your time, knowledge, business connections and expertise are extremely valuable. Share them generously, starting with your formal and informal networking groups. Give speeches. Make presentations. Write articles, letters to the editor and even columns for your local newspaper or trade publication.

- You do not need to restrict the subject matter to your specific business or service. Part of communicating your personal brand as you network is just getting your name and face recognized. The most popular article I have written is called *LinkedIn Tips - Three Free Ideas to Help Employers Find You.* It was not related to my profession, but I received numerous thank-you notes and extensive Internet exposure because of my efforts. I have also been invited to make presentations on LinkedIn to several professional groups.

10. There is no reason you cannot offer some sort of compensation for successful referrals, assuming, of course, that you have analyzed your price structure and determined that it supports the added expense. Furthermore, compensation does not have to mean an actual commission, or even a lot of cash out of your pocket. It can include a gift certificate from your business or a local restaurant, tickets to a cultural event or a charitable donation in the name of the person who provided the referral. However, consider the following points when evaluating referral fees.

- The practice of compensating referrals can be prohibitive to cash-starved businesses struggling to become established.

- Be aware that you may be setting a precedent for those in your networks who would otherwise provide free referrals. Find out what the common practice is for the group, and do not stray too far from the norm.

11. As simple as it may sound, and whatever your reward policy is, you will get far more referrals if you ask for them than if you just wait for them to come to you. The same is true for customer referrals. The key of course is to be tactful and polite, and not to appear overly assertive.

- Adding a brief description of your ideal referral to the end of your 10-second speech will help others provide the type of referrals you are looking for. For example, a benefits consultant might add, "The ideal referral for me is a small business with 25 or more employees."

Creating Dues-free Networking Opportunities:

The goal of the Chamber of Commerce is to act as a business network to promote local businesses. The Chamber of Commerce in my city does a very effective job of carrying out its mission. However, since this book is subtitled 115 Low-cost Ways to Avoid Market Obscurity, I would be remiss if I did not mention that the annual cost for an individual membership would likely be between $150 and $250. Corporate memberships generally start around $250 and can escalate quickly as you grow depending on annual sales, number of employees or other variable factors determined by individual chapters. Furthermore, not all of the cost is tax deductible.

Here are four networking strategies you can implement without incurring dues.

12. Form your own personal networking group. **Every business deals with numerous vendors, bankers, insurance agents, accountants, lawyers, suppliers and so on. Evaluate potential vendor's customer base, and try to select those most similar to your market.** Then trade referrals. Make sure they fully understand your business and marketing objectives.

- Provide each with an ample supply of your business cards, brochures and other promotional literature.

- If some of your vendors fail to reciprocate in promoting your business, do not hesitate to find other vendors who will.

- Vendors who serve other customers and clients in your markets can be a great source of general market intelligence. However, do not ask them to compromise their business ethics by revealing confidential competitor information, and be leery of those who do so voluntarily.

13. Use your burgeoning networking skills to form your own merchants' association, a dues-free personal Chamber of Commerce of sorts. I was recently in a frozen custard store. (Note that if I were making this story up, I would have said a health food store.) As I was leaving, the cashier handed me a 25% coupon. There was nothing unusual about that. However, this coupon was for another retailer selling totally unrelated products. The reality is the second retailer (assume it was a shoe store) would happily hand the identical

coupon to any new customer who walked through their door. This idea is effective because except for the coupon, I would have never given the shoe store a thought.

Many malls and similar retail venues have a merchants' association to promote its members. For example, a common practice is to offer gift certificates that can be redeemed in any member's store. The concept works well for participants in close physical proximity and if marketing partners know and trust you, and are familiar with your product or service.

- Assuming you can obtain the help and support of other members, create an association newsletter or similar forum to keep members informed about matters of common interest like law changes, community events and so forth.

- Above all, never risk your credibility on a questionable referral or by promoting a business you would not patronize yourself.

14. A similar although less formal strategy is employed whenever you see a business prominently displaying other companies' business cards and promotional materials. My barbershop has an entire counter top dedicated to their customers' business cards. I have seen many other companies that post business cards on a bulletin board in their lobby. This type of informal marketing alliance only works with unrelated businesses and only if other merchants reciprocate with

equal enthusiasm. It would be counterproductive for my barbershop to distribute cards or advertise promotions for competing barbers or vendors that sell men's hair products.

15. Another variation of the personal Chamber of Commerce idea is sometimes referred to as the "Buddy Marketing" strategy. Instead of looking for unrelated companies, find ones that are complementary, or whose customers use your product or service. An example would be a sporting goods store joining forces with a health club. The store can offer club members special discounts and promotions on sporting goods products. They can also share mailing lists and even include club promotions in their mailings, electronic distributions and on their website. Perhaps the health club would allow the retailer to demonstrate their products in the club's lobby on occasion.

Let me end the discussion on networking with a quote from Mr. Tom Lewis, an online marketing consultant from "across the pond" who I thought put the whole concept of networking in a rather interesting and concise perspective. He said, "All these new media buzzwords like social networking and technology like LinkedIn are just new ways of complementing (some would say avoiding) personal contact. Get out there and get your face known! Pick up the phone and call some potential clients. Speak at some networking events. Knock on some doors."

Thank you Mr. Lewis, I agree.

Chapter 3

EXTENDING YOUR REACH

The Internet, email and text messaging all became popular within the last 15 years. Earliest examples of written language date to the Bronze Age, around 3000 B.C. I leave to historians, archeologists and Biblical scholars the question of when people first started talking with each other.

Business management columnist Dale Dauten once sarcastically remarked, "It's called a pen. It's like a printer hooked straight to my brain." In a world where it may now be theoretically possible to live your entire life without ever uttering a word or holding a pen, it is easy to forget that communication also includes non-electronic channels. I will say again that effective business communication means conveying your message confidently, concisely and consistently; it is not restricted to any specific medium.

Creating a balance between traditional and Internet-based communications can be a distinct competitive advantage. Some marketing ideas follow.

The Role of Paper in Marketing Your Business:

16. The first marketing investment every businessperson should make is for a professional business card. It is a cheap and effective advertisement. Cards can also serve as instant coupons. Simply sign your name and indicate a percentage or dollar discount the recipient will receive. You can order cards at office supply stores, print shops or online for under 10 cents each, so distribute them generously as you meet new customers and prospects.

Consider the following when designing your business card:

- Avoid high gloss finishes that smear when someone makes notes on them.

- Resist the temptation to print cards yourself. The perforated edges and inferior paper quality will give you away and reflect poorly on your image.

- Business cards have two sides. Use the back to promote your marketing tagline, remind clients of appointments, list your services, etc.

- Stay away from the more common templates. I was once networking with seven people, five of whom had the identical template as me. I ordered new cards that night! A company logo, personal picture or memorable tagline adds distinction.

- There is nothing wrong with ordering free business cards from an online service like VistaPrint. However, their advertisement on the back of your card projects the wrong image. Pay the few extra dollars to have it removed.

- The standard size for business cards in the United States is 3.5 inches by 2 inches. The most popular format is to print cards horizontally along the longer axis. Since I store cards in a binder, if a card is larger than normal it will probably wind up in the trash. Likewise, printing cards vertically along the 3.5-inch axis makes them harder to read once filed. Why do anything to make it more difficult for someone to store and refer to your card? This is not a time to be different. An exception may be if you are in a creative business and want to demonstrate artistic talent on your card.

- The strange picture at the beginning of this chapter is actually my Quick Response or QR Code. A QR Code is a two-dimensional barcode consisting of black modules arranged on a square pattern on a white background. Adding it to your business card makes it readable by QR barcode readers and camera phones. This may be a desirable feature to consider, especially if you are in a technical field. You can create a free QR Code at numerous websites such as http://snapmyinfo.com/blog/how-to-create-a-business-card-qr-code/.

- I have a few personal quirks about business cards. When I see things like 555-456-7890 and JPSmith@xyz.com, I recognize they are phone numbers and email addresses. Do not label them. The one exception is to designate a second number as your cell phone if you are frequently away from your office telephone. Unless there is a compelling reason not to, provide your direct line or extension.

- Finally, decide exactly how you want your card to look, the information to be included, the color, fonts, logo, etc. However, do not be too anxious to hit the "Place Order" button. Save the design and put it aside for a few days. Solicit input from others. Double check your spelling and revisit your design before making a final decision. Everyone wants the perfect card. Nevertheless, reordering new cards because you suddenly realize the red font does not show well on the black background or that your logo is too large can get expensive. I know. I have made both of these mistakes and several others. I am on the fifth or sixth version of my card and plan at least one more "final" change. Learn from my mistakes. As a further precaution, place your initial order for the minimum quantity. You can always reorder if you are satisfied with the finished product.

17. Business cards are only one of many pieces of paper your business uses every day. You also distribute checks, invoices, envelopes, statements, credit card receipts, proposals, cash register tapes, letterhead,

note pads, thank-you notes and so on. Make sure you are getting the full promotional value from every document. Tastefully display your company name, logo and marketing tag line on each document.

18. After you have addressed Ideas #16 and #17, look for opportunities to extend the reach of that paper! Peter J. Patsula, Ph.D. explained why this is important. He said, "Always plan what you are going to sell to your customers next. Never send a package to a customer without including an order form for reorders and sales literature on other products you think they might need." If you pick customer orders from your inventory, (especially mail orders) load the packages and boxes up with product catalogs, special offers, promotions for similar products and so forth. If reorders will be received through the mail, include a postage-paid return envelope. Otherwise, include phone and fax numbers or a website address.

19. It is easy to follow up meetings and customer interactions with email. It is even easier to delete email without reading it. The problem is magnified if you use a domain name that the intended recipient does not recognize, or that is flagged as junk mail by their computer. A handwritten note mailed with a U.S. postage stamp or a phone call can get your message across without breaking the bank. Even if a customer initially contacted you through email, they may find your reply more engaging if you simply pick up the phone.

Using Your Company Vehicles as Marketing Tools:

20. Vehicle graphics on company cars and trucks are inexpensive rolling billboards seen by hundreds of potential customers every day in the neighborhoods and areas where your products or services are purchased and used. Custom magnetic signs can be purchased online, at FedEx Office or franchise operations like Sign-A-Rama for under $100 per pair. Unlike some alternatives, magnetic signs will not depreciate the resale value of your vehicle. Simply remove the signs and reuse them on the replacement vehicle.

21. Other low-cost removable vehicle graphic options to consider are rear window decals and bumper stickers. Depending on the nature of your business and your creative skills, bumper stickers can be given to employees and customers for additional advertising exposure. Order them from the same vendors that sell magnetic signs.

22. A 2007 survey by the American Association of Motor Vehicle Administrators estimated 9.3 million Americans (3.8% of all registered vehicles) had personalized license plates. The study did not report how many of these personalized license plates were used on commercial vehicles. However, if you can subtly communicate your name or message in seven characters or less, try it.

<u>Domain Names and Telephone Numbers:</u>

Andrew Szabo, the "Marketing Chef" and motivational speaker once told me that the average person is bombarded with over 5,000 marketing messages every day. You market to customers and prospects every time they are reminded of your company or products. The question therefore is not how many marketing messages you receive per day, but rather how many you remember the following day and the following week. An obvious example is your phone number. Who can forget 1-800-Flowers?

23. Speaking of telephones, some customers will refuse to deal with voicemail systems. There is nothing you can do to change their behavior. For those who will, provide basic information on your outgoing message including business hours and an emergency contact if appropriate. Let the customer decide how to get in touch with you. They may feel more comfortable with alternative forms of communication such as your website, email or fax.

- Having phones answered by a human during business hours, as opposed to "press 1 for Mary or 2 for Steve," adds a level of personal service probably lacking in some of your competitors.

24. Your domain name is your unique Internet identification, the name by which most of the world will recognize you. **Therefore, you will obviously want to get the best domain name available for your business.** That is an idea that sounds much simpler than it will

likely be in actual practice. Consider the following points:

- Begin by preparing a prioritized list of possible names. Never use an unprofessional sounding domain name unless it is somehow related to or is clearly descriptive of your business. Your name or business name are usually safe bets. Your nickname is not.

- The next step is to search your names on one of the many domain registrars. The largest and best-known registrar is GoDaddy. Others include Network Solutions, Netfirms, and a plethora of smaller firms. Prices vary widely. You will likely use the same vendor to host your website and email, so consider the entire cost of the package, not just the cost of the name registration. Low-cost alternatives are always available. For example, you can have an unlimited number of websites (with email accounts) for less than $5 a month at www.JustHost.com.

- If your preferred name has already been taken, all is not lost. See if it is being used. If not, an active aftermarket exists for domain names. Visit www.Whois.net or www.Better-Whois.com. These free services will show the registrar and, depending on the privacy settings associated with the account, the name and address of the registrant. You can then contact the owner and determine if the domain name is available at a reasonable price. The same services will tell you when the registration expires and (for a small fee) notify you if the registrant fails to renew.

- A cheaper alternative to buying your preferred name on the aftermarket is to construct a similar name, perhaps by simply inserting a hyphen or an abbreviation. Whatever name you choose, try to keep it as short as possible, preferable 12 letters or less. My original domain name was an unmanageable 23 characters long.

- The most widely used domain extension is .com. If that extension has already been taken, other options include .net, .biz, .us and .info. Although originally intended for nonprofit organizations, some commercial ventures use the .org extension. Most registrars will automatically show you other available options if your preferred extension is taken. With the continued expansion of the Internet, the inability to reserve .com does not carry the negative marketing connotations it once did.

- Once you have decided on a domain name and extension, you may want to reserve other available extensions to keep them out of the hands of current and future competitors. For example, I own CFOAmerica.net, CFOAmerica.biz, CFOAmerica.US and CFOAmerica.info. The last two are not currently in use. Additional domain names can be purchased without a hosting package for as little as $10 each, per year.

- Using your domain name for email (rather than a free service like Hotmail or Yahoo) adds professionalism and makes it easier for customers to remember and recognize it. It also further promotes your brand. Most hosting packages include several email accounts. If so, consider individual email accounts for key employees and a general email address like info@yourcompany.com.

25. Even if you have already found a memorable telephone number and catchy domain name, perhaps you can generate additional activity with those of a former competitor. While their value clearly depreciates over time, both means of contact have a shelf life. Adding an old telephone number as a second line or pointing an old web address to your site might generate occasional contacts from customers who are not aware that the company they previously traded with is no longer in business.

- A caution is in order. Investigate the former competitor's reputation, especially why they went out of business. As an obvious example, I would not advise anyone to use Enron's old telephone number. Do not risk your brand through accidental association with a disreputable company. It is likely to generate more complaints and calls from debt collectors than new sales from their former customers.

26. Finally, an obvious but often over-looked prerequisite for any successful company or organization is to be able

to "speak the same language" as their customers and prospects. That phrase has both a figurative and increasingly a literal meaning. For example, a U.S. Census Bureau report titled *Language Use in the United States: 2007* estimated 55 million Americans over the age of five (20% of the population) spoke a language other than English at home. That compared to 23 million in 1980. **Regardless of the nature and location of your market, the ability to communicate across a broad cultural and demographic spectrum can only extend your marketing reach by increasing your potential customer base.** Perform a cost-benefit analysis of bilingual resources that includes your staff, marketing material and basic company forms such as estimates, proposals, invoices and statements. Here are some statistics that might influence your decisions. The social impact of these statistics is profound. You must decide their marketing significance.

- According to the same 2007 Census Bureau report, 35 million Americans over the age of five speak Spanish as their primary language at home. Only half considered themselves able to speak English very well. That percentage is comparable to those who speak Asian and Pacific Island languages at home. With 8 million Americans and a 250% increase since 1980, this is the fastest growing of any language group reported.

- California, Texas, Florida and New York reported a combined Hispanic population of 27 million people, with nine other states having populations in excess of 500 thousand Hispanics.

- A March 22, 2011 article in *USA Today* by David Lieberman had an indication of how prominent the Hispanic culture has become in the American Southwest. That article reported that Texas alone now has 154 Spanish-speaking radio stations, up from 25 ten years ago. The same source reported that the number of Hispanic radio listeners increased by 1.1 million in 2010.

- According to the Kansas City-based Kauffman Foundation, 30% of all new business owners in 2010 were Hispanic, compared to 13% in 1996. Overall, immigrants are more than twice as likely to start businesses as people born in the United States are. These statistics are especially relevant if you have a significant business-to-business component in your value proposition.

British author and lecturer Stuart Wilde summed up the role of every businessperson with a comment similar to Robert Allen's earlier quote. Mr. Wilde said, "Remember that you are a teacher, you are helping people, making them feel safer, taking them from fear to love, from ignorance to knowledge."

Successfully carrying out that role requires that you utilize every communication opportunity and tool at your disposal. It applies to the suggestions of this chapter, and every idea in the book.

Chapter 4

MAKE IT EASY TO BUY

Mark Cuban, billionaire owner of the Dallas Mavericks, clearly explained a simple but universal marketing principle. "Make your product easier to buy than your competition, or you will find your customer buying from them, not you."

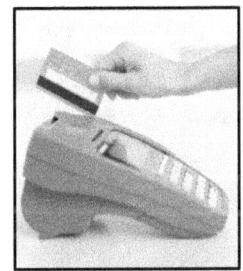

While there are many things that might make it easier or more desirable for customers to do business with you (convenient hours, generous return policies, free coffee, Wi-Fi, gift wrapping and so on) I want to focus on one area, payment options.

Ask yourself, "Do I allow my customers to determine the form of payment most convenient for them, or do I limit options to those most convenient for me?" Here are some marketing ideas to consider.

27. Perhaps the single most important feature making it easy for customers to do business with you is accepting credit and debit cards. According to consumer research consultants America's Research Group, credit cards typically account for 40% of all sales. The public's love of plastic is demonstrated by Starbucks. With an average transaction of only $4, most of their sales are

with a credit, debit or gift card. Numerous studies show that while the vast majority of Americans now have at least one card, most carry less cash since the advent of direct deposit paychecks and debit cards. Many consumers simply no longer carry a checkbook.

The message is clear. Accept card payments or be prepared to wave goodbye to a substantial volume of potential sales. Conversely, adding this convenience will likely translate into increased sales and profits, and perhaps for reasons that have not occurred to you.

Consider the following points:

- Having the ability to pay for unexpected expenditures with a card increases impulse buying and drives up the average dollars per sale.

- Being able to display and advertise card acceptance demonstrates a more professional image and increases business credibility. In his book *Influence - The Psychology of Persuasion,* Robert B. Cialdini reported a study that showed this phenomenon actually increased cash sales by as much as 29%.

- Offering basic merchant services improves cash flow while diminishing the need for daily cash deposits and the risks associated with maintaining large cash balances. It also reduces bad check fees and transfers most of the risk of fraudulent transactions to the issuing bank.

- If you cannot accept credit cards or at least PayPal (refer to Idea #28), you will not be able to compete effectively online.

- When deciding which cards to accept, do not base your decision solely on fees. American Express is well known for charging higher fees. However, it is popular with cardholders because their reward program is considered among the best in the industry.

- Most large banks and a wide variety of other vendors provide the merchant services you will need. Prices vary widely. They can include setup fees, fixed monthly charges and variable costs per transaction. Debit card transaction fees are generally lower than credit cards. Service providers may also require multi-year contractual commitments, with substantial penalties for early termination. Do your research and shop around. Ask merchants in your network about their experiences and for their recommendations. You will probably save money when first starting your business if you opt for a purely variable rate per transaction. **Being locked into paying monthly fixed fees for little or no customer activity is frustrating and expensive.** I learned that lesson the hard way!

The Small Business Authority conducts monthly surveys of business owners on matters such as economic and competitive problems, government regulation, business conditions, and new products. According to a February 1,

2011 report in the *Globe Newswire*, their *January 2011 Market Sentiment Survey* showed that 69% of business owners felt their most important issue for 2011 is increasing sales, while 22% felt the most important issue is reducing costs.

28. PayPal may be an opportunity to address both concerns. Founded in 1998, it was purchased by eBay in 2002 for $1.5 billion. According to PayPal's Press Center, it processed $92 billion of payments (in 24 currencies) and had 94 million accounts in 2010. Originally targeting only online auction payments, PayPal's Merchant Services unit was created in 2003 to provide payment solutions to merchants outside the eBay auction community. The success of this strategic decision has been magnified by a gradual extension of traditional online sales. Once entirely computer based, they now include many point-of-sale transactions for a new generation of cell phone users. For example, PayPal Mobile allows customers to make payments via text messaging.

Eddie Davis, PayPal's Senior Director of Small Business Merchant Services recently said, "In the SBM space, what we've seen is an average lift of 14% higher sales when merchants have added PayPal, and a 23% higher conversion rate than with average credit cards." He went on to say, "And we do all this at a lower cost than a traditional merchant account. There's no set-up fee, and there's no monthly fee for that PayPal central product."

Mr. Davis' advice to small businesses included this, "Merchants and companies need to be thinking about how they can expand the way they accept payment types, how they can convert browsers to buyers. If you think about the mobile phone, that's a new way to reach an audience and take advantage of an impulse buy."

29. I have a monitored home security system. It costs $19.95 per month. The security company mails a bill every month. Several aspects of this practice amaze me. First, the vendor incurs the unnecessary expense of postage and paper. I waste a stamp, check and envelope every month. Do not get me started on the "go green" thing! Furthermore, I suspect being dependent on when customers remember to mail checks makes for less predictable cash flows.

However, there is a far more important and obvious marketing implication involved here. This billing procedure provides every customer with a monthly opportunity to reconsider whether he or she really wants to spend the money! I am going to assume you have implemented the payment options discussed earlier in this chapter. If so, and if your value proposition includes providing recurring services, this situation cries out for an auto-payment system. Offer clients a discount to authorize an automatic credit card charge or bank draft on the first business day of every month. Your customer retention rate will likely improve as billing costs decrease and cash flow becomes far more predictable. Perhaps most important of all, you will make it easier for your clients to do business with you! It is a shining example of what Robert Allen might consider a "never-ending improvement" customer educational opportunity.

- If customers need a monthly invoice, email it to save costs and a trip to the post office.

- Maintaining sensitive financial information like credit card and bank account numbers imposes certain legal obligations and requires an increased level of internal controls to ensure customer security and privacy. Having to announce that your data systems have been compromised or that a laptop containing customer financial records has been stolen are public relations nightmares. I have had my credit card numbers stolen by someone at two different companies, neither of which I will ever use again.

30. The previous idea can be taken an additional step if you sell products on a recurring basis. Assume for example that you sell vitamins and other health supplements. Customers probably purchase in some logical quantity or interval, such as a monthly supply. Offer incentives to authorize you to auto-ship product paid for with a monthly credit card charge or bank draft. Again, customer retention will improve since sales are no longer dependent on them finding time to visit your store. Customers are more likely to continue buying if not effectively forced to reconsider their purchase every 30 days. Finally, you have again simplified and

improved your customers' lives by saving them time and mileage.

31. You have probably heard someone say, "The more things change, the more they stay the same." Layaway payment plans, common since the days of the Great Depression (especially for "big ticket" items like furniture, appliances and jewelry), disappeared from the American retail scene over the past 30 years. They were rendered obsolete by the widespread use of credit cards that allow consumers to "buy now and pay later," a paradigm they much preferred over a "pay now and buy later" scenario.

    However, recent economic challenges led Sears to reintroduce layaway plans in 2006. Kmart, Best Buy and Marshall's soon followed. Here are some points to consider if a layaway plan might increase your sales:

    - National retailers require a fixed down payment (20% seems typical) and charge small service fees. Balances are paid off through scheduled payments over 60 days or so, with delivery only after the final payment. A small penalty may be deducted if an order is canceled. Several chains offer refunds only through store credit. Search the Internet and discuss the matter with merchants in your network to determine fair and reasonable terms for your business and area.

    - The most challenging aspects of layaway plans are the requirements of having an accounting system that can track and bill payments, and an inventory system that can segregate related merchandise. If your systems are not up to these challenges, or if your average retail price is too small, layaway plans are not for you. (P.S. it may be time to invest in a new system!)

I began this chapter with a statement by Mark Cuban on the importance of making it easy for your customers to buy from you. American retailing pioneer F. W. Woolworth put it in even simpler terms. I end the chapter with his comment. He said, "I am the world's worst salesman. Therefore, I must make it easy for people to buy."

So must you!

Chapter 5

ENERGIZING YOUR WORK FORCE

Many companies like to parrot the over-used phrase "our employees are our greatest asset." Far fewer seem to actually believe their own press. **Yet in most businesses, sales and customer service staff are in the best position to favorably influence customer perceptions, resolve issues and identify new marketing opportunities.**

I once made a strategic marketing suggestion to a struggling client. The CEO was sufficiently impressed to write a recommendation that said in part, "CFO America was quite helpful in directing us in some marketing improvements that we could make. We are now in the process of implementing changes that are destined to enhance our financial picture." The suggestion was developed from an employee's comment. Since no one had ever asked for her opinion before I interviewed her, she never volunteered it.

This sort of firsthand market intelligence is a valuable asset; it is up to you to capitalize on it. Here are some ways to help you do just that.

32. Constantly challenge and encourage employees to identify opportunities to enhance marketing efforts,

introduce new products and improve customer service. Maintain an open and direct line of communication through brief but regular staff meetings. Actively solicit their input and try to implement at least one employee suggestion every month. **Reward accepted suggestions in ways they value.** That may mean an employee-of-the-month plaque in the lobby, or a $250 AMEX gift card. If you can spare the labor, a floating holiday is always appreciated. Use your imagination and be willing to experiment as you keep the following quote in mind.

- Mary Kay Ash, the founder of Mary Kay Cosmetics once said, "Everyone has an invisible sign hanging from their neck saying, make me feel important. Never forget this message when working with people." Her quote applies to both customers and employees. For that reason, make sure every employee fully understands how important the accomplishment of his or her individual goals is to achieving overall company success. Publicly praise them when they accomplish a major milestone toward achieving those goals.

33. Do not assume every employee knows all they need to know about your products, services, company policies or even the basics of sales and customer service. **Make the effort to ensure they are adequately trained on all critical aspects of your business.** Simply teaching them to up sell by always asking the equivalent of the fast food industry's standard question, "Do you want fries

with that order?" will go a long way toward increasing average customer purchases.

Why is this important? Alan J. Zell, author and retail marketing expert says, "Every business needs more business. That is an accepted fact. The unaccepted fact is that most businesses don't use all the opportunities available that will bring them additional business. When one looks for additional business, the primary goal should center around getting second sales. What are second sales and why are they important? Second sales are add-on sales, repeat sales and sale by referral. They are important because they are much less expensive to get than first sales."

- If you would like to see Mr. Zell's advice in practice, try leaving a shoe store without being asked if you need extra laces, polish and a few extra pairs of socks to go with your new shoes. It cannot be done!

34. I talked earlier about the importance of networking. If there are too many networking opportunities for one person, have a key employee join a group or two. It will be a growth experience for them and it demonstrates your trust and appreciation. It will also give you the opportunity to grow your business through their network contacts.

35. I can still remember my excitement over 35 years ago when, having just graduated college, I brought my first business card home and presented it to my father. I do not know who was prouder, my dad or me. I also gave

copies to everyone I knew, and probably strangers I passed on the street. However, what I attributed to pride, my employer probably chalked up to that cheap advertising I talked about in Chapter 3. Order business cards for all your permanent employees. They are sure to hand them out generously.

36. Offer substantial discounts to employees. While it will probably not generate significant sales or gross profits, it will generate goodwill. More importantly, it encourages employees to use and demonstrate your products in front of customers, family and friends. This is especially applicable in retail businesses that sell consumer products like clothing and jewelry.

37. It is a sad fact that most businesses cannot afford to compensate valuable employees as much as they would like to. Providing a competitive benefits package is even more difficult for small businesses. In a challenging economy, many do well just to be able to offer continued employment. Here is a variation of the previous idea that may help employers in your area while generating significant sales for you. Offer discounts or special services to someone else's employees. I once worked for a 400-employee company that arranged (at my suggestion) a pickup and delivery service by a local dry cleaner. Another employer provided a weekly car cleaning service. Since employees paid for either service as they used them, both examples created a cost-free benefit from the employers' perspective. The services created value since they allowed employees to complete personal

errands they would otherwise have to address on their own time. More to the point, these examples also presented a large one-stop customer base for the service providers.

- This strategy may work especially well as a means of extending a business-to-business relationship to your customers' employees. For example, if you repair their employer's computers, employees will already be familiar with your service and reputation. Offer them a discount for home computer service, especially if they can save you a trip by bringing personal computers to work.

38. **Finally, always tie incentive compensation and individual employee goals to the specific behavior that will accomplish your marketing goals.** A former employer of mine once ran a promotion offering bonuses for all increased sales. The problem was they were already losing money on some products, primarily because those products were underpriced. When sales of the loss leaders increased, the added cost of bonuses produced a "double whammy" on their bottom line.

- Do you see why I keep stressing the importance of accountability or knowing your numbers? If your goal is to increase high margin sales, offer bonuses only on high margin products. If the goal is to increase the average sale per customer, offer employee incentives only for sales above a predetermined minimum. It will be more difficult to administer an incentive program like this, but the bottom line impact will be well worth it.

I will end the chapter on *Energizing Your Work Force* with a quote from John Willard Marriott, the late founder of the hospitality chain that bears his name. Mr. Marriott summarized the ultimate reason why every business must energize their work force. He said, "Motivate them, train them, care about them, and make winners out of them. They'll treat the customers right. And if customers are treated right, they'll come back."

Given Marriott International's $11.7 billion of revenue and 34% return on equity in 2010, I must assume Marriott employees are still treating customers right, 25 years after his passing.

Chapter 6

BECOMING A RECOGNIZED EXPERT

There is an old axiom in marketing that a prospect does not become a customer until a vendor touches them seven times. Touches or interactions involve every tool in your marketing quiver, including media advertising, direct mail, networking, window and point-of-sale displays,  telemarketing, email campaigns, web based marketing, trade shows and face-to-face meetings.

The axiom is no doubt based on a common sense assumption. **Consumers prefer to do business with people and companies they know, like and trust.** The question every business must answer is how to initiate and sustain the process without crossing the fine line of being perceived as just another pushy or (worse yet) desperate sales person.

Event-based Marketing:

Event-based marketing will allow you to interact with potential customers and encourage them to seek you out for your knowledge and expertise. Since there are several event-based promotional ideas presented here and in Chapter 12, I will begin with a few tips to increase their attendance and effectiveness.

A. There are several free event-listing sites available on the Internet should you wish to open your events to the public. Most allow business promoters to coordinate announcements and listings through Facebook and Twitter. Online event-listing websites include:

- EventSync

- EventBrite

- PlanCast

- Zvents

B. A drawing for a free gift certificate, an autographed copy of your latest book (more about that in Idea #51) or some other valuable prize will encourage attendees to stay for the entire presentation.

C. Promotional material must identify specific customer problems and promise real solutions. Make sure information presented at the event closely matches those promises. They are what drew attendees. It is unlikely that disappointed prospects, frustrated at not hearing the promised solutions, will become your customer.

D. The main point of your presentation is what the audience wants to hear, not what you want to tell them. Get to it quickly.

E. You want your audiences' undivided attention. Therefore, present only a cryptic outline on slides and handouts at the event. Otherwise, attendees could have read the presentation at home and saved the trip.

F. Attendees will expect a commercial. Hold it for the last or next to last slide.

G. Finally, track new business and contacts from every event. Several small businesses I know consider free seminars to be by far their most effective marketing tool.

Here are some specific event-based marketing ideas.

39. Look for speaking engagements to demonstrate your knowledge, expertise and professional leadership. You also want to build awareness of your products and services, highlighting their functionality and competitive advantages. Business and social groups such as the Lions, Rotary, garden clubs and Chamber of Commerce usually have guest speakers at every meeting. Do not overlook local public service radio and television programs as speaking opportunities.

40. Hold free meetings, seminars or webinars. I am not talking about locking prospects in a room and brow beating them into submission, or presenting a thinly disguised infomercial. We have all suffered through a few of those! I am talking about a free and open sharing of your knowledge and expertise. Jimmy Stewart said, "Never treat your audience as customers. Treat them as partners." Focus on solving real problems for those partners, not selling your products or services.

41. Collaborate with experts in other fields to share their skill sets. Have an attorney talk about relevant legal issues. Have a CPA discuss tax saving opportunities or an insurance agent explain the basics of business liability insurance. Again, there is no need to limit topics to a narrow band around your business. The litmus test of any agenda is merely this: are the topics interesting and relevant enough to entice your target audience to attend the meeting?

   - The best forum for this type of collaborative event marketing might be a panel discussion featuring experts from several disciplines.

   - Develop a list of your top 10 or 20 prospective clients or customers. Consider inviting their owners or executives to participate in your panel discussion. It will give you an opportunity to learn more about their needs.

42. Make good use of your formal and informal networks in promoting events, identifying speakers and defining topics. Tell members of your networking groups that you are available and eager to speak, and would welcome their participation. Ask every speaker for a brief resume for use in advanced promotions and in their introduction. Have them promote the event to their customers and contacts.

   - Get a list of their invitees. Have attendees sign in with contact information and add them to your mailing list.

- Crosscheck attendees with the advanced registration list. Then send a "sorry you couldn't attend" message to everyone who registered but failed to show up. Provide copies of meeting handouts and summaries, or refer them to your website as discussed in Idea #47.

43. Subject relevance for your meeting is critical. Present solutions for problems your audience is facing today, even if your advice allows them to solve those problems without buying from you. Remember, your goal is that the meeting provides one of several contacts. It is to draw prospects into a process that will eventually result in sales for your company. Make a good impression and some of your audience will give you that opportunity. You will also benefit from word of mouth advertising as attendees share your information and solutions with others.

   - Many business people believe word of mouth advertising is their most effective form of communication. It is certainly among the cheapest. However, what makes it so effective is that from the message recipient's point of view, the person telling them about your business solutions probably already has a high trust factor that other forms of marketing can only hope to achieve.

   - Support word of mouth advertising with a generous distribution of business cards, bios and other promotional materials.

44. Subject matter does not need to be highly technical or even glamorous to be relevant. Several national home improvement centers hold seminars on how to design and install basic home improvements like flooring, wallpaper, landscaping and so forth. Guess who just happens to sell all the supplies the homeowner will need to complete the do-it-yourself project? I recently heard of a home cleaning service that held a series of meetings on proper cleaning techniques. After a few months, they had more new customers than they could accommodate.

- As the cleaning service example clearly illustrates, you will frequently have attendees who decide it is easier or simply more efficient to retain you to solve their problems, even if they are capable of doing so themselves.

45. Becoming accredited or qualified to provide Continuing Professional Education (CPE) credits to accountants, lawyers, realtors and many other licensed professionals involves time and perhaps some costs. However, if your target customers are required to obtain CPE, it will give your seminars a distinct advantage over your competition, especially if held near the end of that profession's licensing period. I attend a monthly seminar sponsored by a national consulting and executive search firm. Although held in a large hotel, it is routinely over-subscribed by several hundred CPAs anxious for two hours of free CPE. It also provides the sponsor with a large talent pool for future assignments and placements.

- Visit the National Registry of CPE Sponsors, a program offered by the National Association of State Boards of Accountancy to recognize CPE program sponsors for CPAs. Search the Internet for the recognized credentialing organizations and educational requirements of other professions in your target market.

- Consider having attendees visit your website for CPE certificates.

46. Follow up meetings, seminars and demonstrations by thanking attendees and soliciting their feedback, especially their suggestions on topics for future events. Make the communication as personal as possible. For that reason, the U.S. mail or a phone call is more distinctive than an email. A handwritten note is preferable to a form letter. Whatever you decide to do, it is one more opportunity for you to touch prospective customers in an unobtrusive manner.

Here are three additional ways to make your events more appealing to potential customers while stretching your limited marketing budget.

47. Drive traffic to your website, save money and "go green" all in one process. Earlier, I suggested presenting only a cryptic handout at an event. Its main purpose is to keep the audience focused by providing a convenient form for their note taking. However, you can post a complete set of slides, notes and other supporting material following the meeting. That way attendees can

print only what they need, and at their cost. Encourage attendees to share the material with friends and business associates.

- Make sure your company name, logo and contact information are prominently displayed. Use an inalterable format like a .pdf file or a password-protected document.

48. Have business partners co-sponsor events. They can share in the cost of promotion, refreshments, seminar materials, etc. Make sure you acknowledge their support on promotional announcements, slides, handouts and introductions.

49. Restaurants sometimes offer free use of rooms (especially during off-peak times) for your meetings as a way of promoting themselves. It is a win-win for all concerned, so ask them! I have held seminars in Starbucks restaurants. Attendees bought their own coffee. Churches and community groups may also be a source of free or low-cost facilities for your seminars and meetings. Be an appreciative tenant.

Publish or Perish:

The pressure to publish original works in order to compete for tenured positions in academia gave rise to the phrase "publish or perish." In the past, authoring books and papers to establish expertise may have been the easy part. It also required finding publishers. In the case of books, it forced authors to incur significant upfront expenses. For example, publishers might charge setup fees and have a minimum first printing of 1,000 books. Since the average book only sells about 700 copies, many undoubtedly collected dust in the author's attic until given away as presents or discarded.

The old publishing paradigms have been completely redefined in the information age ushered in by the Internet. Here are two ideas available to everyone at minimal or no cost.

50. Publish your seminar content, articles, papers, press releases and anything else you have written on free Internet article marketing services. You can find my LinkedIn article, the material presented in Appendix I, and several other articles I have written on these websites.

- Internet article marketing services include:

    a. Buzzle

    b. Digg

    c. EzineArticles

    d. GoArticles

    e. Reddit

    f. Scribd

    g. StumbleUpon

h. Uber Articles

- Keep in mind that the average Internet viewer is either very busy, somewhat impatient, or both. They are not searching for an online English translation of Tolstoy's *War and Peace*. They are looking for interesting, concise articles that provide relevant content in a reader-friendly format. Tailor your writing style to match that profile for maximum hits.

- Every business has certain words and phrases that potential customers are likely to use in search engines when looking for your products or services. These words or phrases are called keywords. For example, assume I operate a catering service. Relevant keywords might include catering, caterers, event planning, cater, caterer, caterer for weddings, menu catering, and so on. Actually, my example includes eight out of the top ten most searched words and phrases related to catering in my local area during the previous month. I found them using Google's Keyword Tool, which is available free online. If my business was located in suburban Dallas, I might also add the words Dallas area or Texas to each phrase.

- **Making all online material keyword rich therefore optimizes or increases the chances that potential customers will find you in their search.** For that reason, this process is often referred to as search engine optimization, or simply SEO. Some experts tell us including keywords in the title and the first 90 characters is especially important for best results. Keywords should be used throughout the article, but without affecting its readability. A "keyword density" of up to 5% is the norm.

- Include a brief "About the Author" section at the end of each manuscript. Your biography should establish your subject matter expertise. Including a link to your website also improves search engine results as discussed in the previous bullets.

51. Here is a question to consider. **What would it do for your professional credibility and promotional efforts if you could hold up your own book every time you spoke in public?** Even if you never sold a single copy, but just displayed the books and handed them out as door prizes, I suspect it would provide a tremendous marketing advantage over your less prolific and linguistically talented competitors. Let me be clear. I am not talking about creating the great American novel or writing something that knocks John Grisham and Dan Brown off the New York Times Best Seller List. I should also caution that if your intention is to generate enough royalties to quit your day job, following this idea is not likely to accomplish that goal.

I am talking about authoring a paperback book that demonstrates and shares your considerable body of knowledge and skills, and that is written and packaged in such a way that you can be proud to hold it up in front of any audience. Its primary purpose is that of a marketing tool to promote the sale of your products and services by establishing you as a recognized expert in your field. However, think of it as a marketing cost, not a potential profit center.

There are numerous print-on-demand companies available online to authors. Most offer publishing packages ranging from free (and therefore very basic) Do-It-Yourself to a variety of optional services such as cover design, professional editing, eReader formats and distribution assistance. Each option adds a layer of fees, and can very quickly disqualify this idea from my "low-cost" criteria. I suggest you avoid companies that charge significant fixed setup fees, impose minimum orders or do not provide online marketing assistance. Other variables include pricing strategies for paperbacks and eReaders, and royalty options.

Amazon's CreateSpace is one of the best-known print-on-demand companies. Its website was designed to walk novice authors through a self-publishing process. It allows you to easily design and publish professional-looking paperback or hardcover books with no minimum orders, and at single copy prices that can literally be less than a Venti cappuccino at Starbucks. It also offers several free online marketing portals, allowing different pricing strategies in each.

Here is how Amazon describes their subsidiary. "CreateSpace provides one of the easiest, fastest, and most economical ways to distribute your content to millions of potential customers on Amazon.com and other channels. Media formats supported through CreateSpace include books, DVDs, CDs, video downloads, and Amazon MP3s. With the CreateSpace manufacturing-on-demand model, your products will be produced as customers order, so you don't have to make an up-front investment in inventory. Plus, CreateSpace takes care of the customer service and order fulfillment on your online retail orders, so you can focus on promoting your titles."

Here is a final thought on Idea #51. Unless you are fortunate enough to find a solution for world hunger, there is probably nothing you will do in your career that deserves to be promoted more than publishing your first book. Use every marketing tool at your disposal to promote it!

- Issue a press release (Idea #54).

- Publicize it on your blog (Idea #52), social media network (Chapter 7), and website.

- Promote the book within your network groups and to your customers by throwing a launch party. If you have contacts with newspapers or other local media outlets, invite them as well. Consider donating a portion of the event's book sale proceeds to a local charity. The charity will in turn promote the launch party to their network of volunteers and supporters.

- Finally, distribute your book as holiday presents to your key clients and prospects.

Other Internet-based Communication Channels:

52. Hollywood has obliged me by producing a movie to illustrate the next marketing idea. The 2009 movie *Julie and Julia* recounts the experiences of Julie Powell as portrayed by actress Amy Adams. It tells the true story of Powell's 2004 experience writing a daily blog of recipes from Julia Child's book *Mastering the Art of French Cooking*. Ms. Powell's personal commitment was to prepare and discuss 524 recipes in 365 days, all in her tiny apartment kitchen. It was as she described it a "deranged assignment" that was often overwhelming. Early on, the only feedback Powell received about her blog was critical posts from her own mother. She had no idea whether anyone else was reading her content. After a few months, the blog slowly caught on. It eventually became a great American success story. Her blog posts were later compiled into her first book, *Julie & Julia: 365 Days, 524 Recipes, 1 Tiny Apartment Kitchen*.

A blog is simply a website where businesses and individuals share information about marketing, branding and other matters of common interest. Blogs can include videos and pictures. Most are interactive, allowing visitors to leave comments and share posted information with others. Blogging is a powerful and flexible educational tool. Use it to demonstrate your subject matter expertise and communicate your products and services to a wide audience.

The idea of starting a blog for your business is especially appealing since several well-known vendors (for example, WordPress and Blogger.com) are available to you free of charge. These services are user friendly, flexible and can be optimized to enhance search engine results. Remember the following points in your blogging:

- Develop a consistent writing style, generally limiting each post to 400 to 600 words.

- Be consistent in your reporting schedule. For example, my blog is updated with fresh content every Monday, Wednesday and Friday morning. My blog can be viewed at www.CFOAmerica.biz.

- If you know in advance that you will be unavailable at your normal reporting time, you can upload your post and schedule it for automatic release.

- Be engaging and invite readers to post comments to your blog. However, monitor those comments for inappropriate content. WordPress, for example, will not show reader comments until you approve them.

- As you engage with others, respect their beliefs and opinions. Avoid sounding too negative or critical, especially when discussing your competition.

- Again, recognize that blogging can initially be somewhat frustrating. You will probably question if anyone is reading your content. Do not give up too quickly. Remember Julie Powell's experience and ultimate success. Bon appétit!

53. Participating in message board discussions is another free way to raise your profile within your community of current and potential customers and in your area of expertise. A message board is nothing more than an online discussion forum where people with common interests and knowledge exchange information by posting questions and answers, along with other relevant comments. Messages usually require approval from a moderator before being visible. They can be archived indefinitely.

Answering questions on message boards gets you recognized as an expert. Asking questions gathers valuable information. The quote from Tom Lewis in Chapter 2 came to me in response to a question I posted on a message board. Answering and asking questions both help grow followers for your social media sites as discussed in the following chapter.

- Message boards are available for virtually every industry, profession and product. For example, Intuit hosts "Accountants Community for QuickBooks Practitioners and Accounting Professionals" where experienced users of their hugely popular QuickBooks software ask and answer questions. In essence, Intuit supplements their customer support function with participants' expertise. Search the Internet or ask your network contacts for message boards relevant to your business and expertise. Then contribute your knowledge frequently.

- LinkedIn Answers and Yahoo Answers message boards, like many others, rate responders by how many participants "Like" their answers and how often their response is selected as the best answer. This is a highly desirable feature and a real feather in your professional cap.

- Include a link to your website in your message board signature.

Press Releases:

54. You have probably figured out by now that I love to use quotes and old sayings. Have you heard the one, "there is no such thing as bad publicity?" Lindsay Lohan and Charlie Sheen might disagree with that. So do I.

Press releases must be newsworthy, interesting and engaging across a wide readership. Nevertheless, if something happens in your business that meets those criteria, free publicity is hard to argue with, especially since you are sure to write nice things about yourself. Examples of newsworthy events include a new product, a recent expansion or new facility, a speaking engagement, sponsorship of a charity event, a professional award or recognition and again, publishing a book. You might also consider issuing a press release if you land a major new client or contract. Be sure to email the client an advanced copy of the press release. Ask them to signify their approval by return email.

A press release is nothing more than a short news article, typically three or four paragraphs long. Here are some tips to help you get started:

- Write in a journalistic style, beginning with an attention-grabbing headline.

- The first paragraph should provide an overview of the news item and explain why it is important. It should sound exciting to a general audience.

- The next paragraph typically provides background on the purpose or benefits of your products or services.

- The final paragraph should be a description of your company. Include "For more information contact:" as the last sentence.

- Minimize the use of highly technical and industry-specific jargon that might confuse the general public.

- Be prepared to answer questions and even defend press release statements. Local newspapers and the trade press might want a more in-depth understanding of your news than provided in the press release. While working for a large national company, a financial rating agency once informed us that the results of their new "multi-variant discriminant analysis" showed we were a very solid company. Our Public Relations Director gleefully issued a press release, quoting the rating agency verbatim. Unfortunately, we soon learned he had no clue what a multi-variant discriminant analysis was. For a few short days, I was his best friend.

- You can find numerous press release templates and suggestions online. One free and valuable resource is http://www.theprdoc.com, a website by public relations expert Jim Bowman. Jim is a very talented and knowledgeable network contact of mine.

- If you still feel uncertain about how to write or distribute a press release, Amazon lists 13 software programs under $30 each.

- Target media outlets including local newspapers, trade publications, and television and radio stations.

- Numerous online newswire directories that specialize in providing business related content will publish your press release. Some provide basic services free, while charging for enhanced services like including your logo. Others charge for every press release. This industry has a history of converting from free to fee-based services, so some pre-release investigation will be necessary. As of this writing, examples of free services you may wish to experiment with include:

a. i-Newswire

b. NewswireToday

c. PRToday

d. PRZoom

- As discussed in Idea #50, make sure your headlines and press releases are keyword rich to optimize search engine results and increase exposure.

- Finally, distribute press releases through your own blog, websites and other social media platforms discussed in the next chapter.

55. Lastly, reprints of press releases, blog posts, articles written by or about you and even your "best answers" are excellent testimonials to your expertise and prominence in your industry. Toot your own horn by periodically distributing copies to customers and prospects. Include them in customer mailings, mail orders, newsletters, marketing packets and similar material. Always keep a supply in your lobby.

- Including a professional photograph with published material puts a human face on your business.

- While distributing marketing materials as email attachments is easy and cost efficient, it also increases the risk that recipients will not open the email due to security concerns over computer viruses often transmitted in attachments. For that reason, including critical points in the actual body of your email may be preferable.

Chapter 7

WORD OF MOUTH IS NOW GLOBAL

Through your efforts to become a recognized expert in your field, you will accumulate an ever-growing body of material (articles, papers, program notes, research material, PowerPoint presentations and so on) that  can serve as content for the next group of ideas.

Social media marketing is all the rage. Embattled TV star Charlie Sheen set a Guinness world record on March 2, 2011. He reached 1 million Twitter followers in just 25 hours and 17 minutes. It took Mr. Sheen four days to reach 2 million followers. It remains to be seen whether he will catch Lady Gaga, who currently "leads the pack" with approximately 10 million Twitter followers.

Social media has influenced national elections and at least one guest host selection for *Saturday Night Live*. Viewers of Super Bowl XLV learned the Chevrolet Cruze can now read Facebook newsfeed content in real-time, affording drivers "the ability to send status updates and stay connected to social platforms." Exactly what those social platforms are is unclear as of this writing; however, speculation is that it will likely include Twitter.

Moreover, as events of recent years have proved, totalitarian governments in many parts of the world think it is easier to control civil unrest online than in their streets. The first casualties of politically embarrassing protests are often these same social networking sites. Egyptian activist and Google executive Wael Ghonim was a leader of the early 2011 uprising that toppled President Hosni Mubarak. He told CNN, "I want to meet Mark Zuckerberg one day and thank him. I'm talking on behalf of Egypt. This revolution started online. This revolution started on Facebook." I was fascinated to learn that the U.S. State Department starting tweeting in Arabic during the crisis.

The socio-economic and political impact of social media is a source of inspiration for some and fear for others. The statistics are impressive for all.

Let me provide a working definition of the term social media marketing. It relies on Internet platforms to distribute content that attracts attention and encourages readers to share your message with their social network. That sharing or broad distribution of your message is, in my opinion, the essence of social media marketing. **As the title of this chapter suggests, it is truly a modern day extension of traditional word of mouth advertising on a global scale.** As I previously said, a marketing message received from someone you know and trust carries the tacit understanding that the messenger considers it interesting and relevant to you, and probably that they believe it to be valid.

Some of the more popular social media platforms are:

A. Facebook

B. Foursquare

C. LinkedIn

D. MySpace

E. Twitter

F. YouTube

Each has a somewhat distinctive set of demographics such as average age, gender, education level, membership size, U.S. and global traffic volume, length of average visit and so on. Visit www.alexa.com to find the best matches for your target market.

Whatever platforms are chosen, they provide incoming or backlinks to your website and blog. This improves search engine results since the number of backlinks is an indication of the popularity and importance of a website.

Businesses use social media marketing to increase brand awareness and promote products and services. Businesses also receive feedback from customers and potential markets. Perhaps the best analogy I have heard was a comparison to a large, porous funnel. The various platforms cast a wide net to gather many followers into the funnel. As you continue to provide valuable and interesting content and develop relationships, some of those followers will eventually progress through the narrowing funnel to become customers and sources of referrals. Others will fall away.

Because these social media websites are available free to everyone with Internet access, they present inexpensive and powerful platforms for small businesses to get market feedback and conduct targeted marketing campaigns on a local, regional, national or even global basis.

How popular is social media marketing? I got a sense of the interest it generates when I searched Amazon for the phrase "Facebook marketing" and got 452 results. I got 1,618 hits when I searched "social media marketing." Products included a cornucopia of books and videos priced up to $1,200, and included 137 hits of "For Dummies" books alone.

Perhaps the real surprise is why there were not more results. According to Goldman Sachs, Facebook has over 600 million active users (defined as those who log on at least three times a week) including President Obama and Queen Elizabeth. Perhaps buoyed by the 2010 movie *The Social Network*, that is a 20% increase in just six months. According to LinkedIn's Press Center, they have over 100 million users speaking six languages in more than 200 countries. They add a new user every second. In September 2010, Co-founder Evan Williams said Twitter is averaging 90 million tweets per day. They are gaining 370,000 new accounts daily, with 16% of them starting the service on mobile devices. I could go on, but I am sure you get the idea.

Social media marketing is simply too large to ignore, especially if your target market is under the age of 40, affluent and highly educated. It demands attention because of its size, growth trends and cost efficiency when compared to alternative marketing channels.

This chapter's suggestions should be obvious by now.

56. Evaluate social media marketing as a platform to build brand awareness and share content with your customers and target market. Use it as a vehicle to provide your customers with a voice. Encourage feedback and ask questions of your followers. Social media marketing is all about consistent communication in channels selected by your markets. Do not fall victim to the common misconception that it is about technology! Moreover, remember that ultimately you are connecting with individuals, not faceless companies and organizations.

    • Individuals all have birthdays, families, homes, hobbies and other personal characteristics and interests that they will occasionally mention online. Apply what Dale Carnegie said about making friends by being interested in other people rather than by trying to get people interested in you. Remember the personal stuff!

    • It is very likely that you will eventually attract hundreds and even thousands of followers on your social media platforms. It will not be possible (or even advisable) to attempt to develop relationships with all of your connections, especially since many will be in distant areas that effectively disqualify them as prospects. However, for those online connections that are realistic customer prospects, cultivating an offline relationship will greatly increase sales opportunities.

- Try to exhibit a conversational style, but keep in mind that your conversations will be online, and therefore accessible to virtually the entire planet.

57. If you decide to move forward with social media marketing, the next crossroad you will come to in your analysis and evaluation is whether to do everything yourself or hire experts. Make an informed decision. There are plenty of free or low-cost educational resources available to you. Begin with an Internet search or by spending a few dollars on one of those 1,618 books and videos. Talk to your social media savvy friends and associates, perhaps starting with your "screenage" children. Having done my research, I decided that while I could muddle through the maze myself, the time saved and professionalism gained by hiring a consultant was worth the small investment. I should also mention that I met my social media consultants at a free seminar they sponsored.

- Look at what competitors and others in your area are doing. Make a list of what you like and dislike about each. Remember, imitation is the sincerest form of flattery. In this situation, it may also be the cheapest.

58. Develop a social media plan that includes target dates and milestones. It should incorporate several platforms with a consistent message and theme or look. Each platform should be linked to your website or blog. Fred Campos, a social media expert and founder of FunCitySocialMedia likes to compare social media marketing to a three-legged stool. Following his analogy, I ultimately selected Twitter, Facebook and LinkedIn as my three legs. Again, visit www.alexa.com to find the best matches for your target market.

I also have two websites, one of which is the WordPress blog that I mentioned earlier. The other is a "landing pad" that presents a three-minute video and invites viewers to opt-in to my mailing list and receive a free publication that explains my services and business approach. It can be found at www.CFOAmerica.net.

My social media platforms always carry a summary of blog postings. To the extent possible, Twitter, Facebook and both websites have a similar look as to color scheme, graphics and narrative theme. While LinkedIn is far more limiting in its graphic design options, it does allow your logo and picture. And it is hard to argue with free!

- Your followers can greatly magnify the distribution of anything you post by making it available to their contacts. They do that on Facebook by simply clicking the "Like" button. On LinkedIn, they recommend you. On Twitter, they "retweet" your comments. Whatever it is called, encourage your following to share your content for maximum exposure.

59. I confess that I have been slow to incorporate YouTube into my social media marketing arsenal. That is probably to my detriment. Although you can post pictures and links to videos on most social media platforms, YouTube is specifically designed as a video sharing site. Many people therefore think of it primarily as a source of entertainment. However, YouTube is currently the most popular search engine. The company was founded in 2005 and bought by Google in 2006. YouTube reported it had in excess of 2 billion downloads per day in May of 2010.

     YouTube is free, and has many practical applications for small businesses. You can prepare and upload amateur videos with most cell phones and digital cameras. Here are seven YouTube tips:

     • If you believe a picture is worth a thousand words, YouTube videos may be priceless. Your videos can be used to demonstrate your products in action, showcase samples of your work, record customer testimonials, address frequently asked questions and serve almost any customer educational purpose that arises. Videos can be made more user-friendly and accessible through the auto-caption feature added in early 2010. Captions can then be translated into over 50 languages. This means the hearing-impaired and non-English speaking audiences will have access to the information and marketing messages contained in your videos.

- YouTube allows users to set up personal channels similar to home pages. This affords the opportunity to present video messages in a customized environment consistent with your brand's use of colors, logos, marketing taglines and so on. Channels can also display user data including contact information, web addresses and pictures. Finally, users can organize videos in logical groups or sequences through playlists.

- While YouTube is the largest video sharing site, it is not the only one. Consider posting your videos (and potentially reaching additional markets) on other sites such as Bing, Dailymotion (a French-based company second only to YouTube) and Metacafe.

- As previously discussed in Idea #50, make the title and description of your videos keyword rich to achieve maximum exposure through search engine optimization.

- Video titles tend to invite greater attention if they are in the form of a question, "how to" advice, self-help tips or lists (for example, *Five Ways to Increase Your Sales*).

- Use your other social media outlets to cross-promote YouTube videos.

- Again, study what your competition is doing on YouTube. Look at a few viral or most popular videos to see what characteristics make them popular. Tasteful humor is a common trait. Adapt the lessons learned to your own situation.

60. Even if you use outside assistance to design and develop your social media platforms, generating fresh content remains your responsibility. Quite simply, no one knows more about your business than you do. Demonstrate that fact by sharing the body of material you accumulated in becoming a recognized expert. However, resist the temptation to share it all at once. **Building a following in cyberspace is a marathon, not a sprint.** As with blogging, develop a consistent conversational style and reporting pattern.

Here are a few pointers to get the most social media mileage out of your content and maximize its effectiveness:

- If you have a document with multiple bullet points, break it into several posts.

- End each post by briefly telling readers what to expect in your next entry, and when it will be published.

- Most content can be reformatted and repurposed as appropriate. For example, press releases and articles can be posted on Facebook and other sites as well as your blog. A 1,200-word article can provide a lot of content at 140 characters per tweet. Facebook status update fields have a 420-character limit. LinkedIn has a 700-character limit. Other social networks each have similar limits. With a little practice, you will probably find, as I did, that communicating your message within those limits is usually quite easy to accomplish.

- You can supplement your original content with relevant quotes and articles written by others, or simply pass along helpful advice and suggestions you come across in your daily business. Numerous websites provide extensive quotes on every business subject imaginable. As an example, visit www.brainyquote.com.

- Timely material can be re-circulated or retweeted periodically.

- Unless supporting a particular point of view is a deliberate part of your branding and marketing strategy, avoid expressing religious and political opinions or supporting controversial agendas that might alienate potential customers and followers.

- Have several people proofread and review your content. Check your pride of authorship at the door. Do not be afraid to use someone who will look you in the eye and tell you if you have "an ugly baby." My son's unbridled desire to correct his father makes him an extremely effective proofreader. Another friend's frank comments often bruise my ego. I typically stew about them for a day, and then incorporate most of his suggestions.

- No one cares about trivial matters like what you ate for dinner unless you are a food critic or Kim Kardashian. Maintain an air of business decorum and professionalism in your social media platforms. Excessive personal or inappropriate content posted on business platforms will only encourage followers to unfollow you.

- There are numerous social networking tools available free online to help you monitor and simultaneously update multiple sites such as Twitter, Facebook and LinkedIn. Those tools currently include:

a. Tweetdeck

b. Hootsuite

c. Ping.fm

Most also provide upgraded versions for a fee. It is a truism of any free-market system that whenever a product or service becomes an undifferentiated commodity, those offering it can only compete on price. It is therefore inevitable in the fast-paced world of social media that as soon as someone develops a new Internet-based service, someone else will figure out how to make money by offering it free. Periodically ask your social media active friends and network contacts whether they are aware of any new tools.

- The ultimate purpose of social media marketing is to build business relationships. All relationships require two-way communication. Do not get so consumed in posting content that you neglect to respond to direct messages or DMs. Try to establish a dedicated time every day to answer your DMs.

61. Finally, having gone through the effort to develop content, create a social media marketing program and build a following, do not fail to promote Twitter, Facebook etc. on outgoing email signatures, business cards, letterhead, websites, and promotional materials.

- Every media platform should be used to promote all the others. For example, you should occasionally send a tweet inviting followers to "Like" your Facebook Fan page, and use Facebook and Twitter to announce new posts on your blog.

- Provide a direct link to your blog and social media platforms whenever possible. For example, my outgoing email signature ends with, "Please click on the links below to read our blog or to follow us on Facebook & Twitter."

This chapter presents many new challenges for the already overworked small businessperson. Let me end with one more. Future Vision Web Services made this observation: "Most of today's market leaders are those companies who had the foresight to recognize the changing landscape in today's modern business world. The new business battleground has been very cruel to those companies that have fallen behind the curve."

Do not allow the rapidly evolving landscape of social media marketing to keep you from realizing the full potential of your business.

INTERNET MARKETING BASICS

Businesses have long used the Internet as a one-way communication channel to inform and educate customers about their products, prices, locations and hours. One-way communication is no longer sufficient, even for small businesses.

Here are some ways to expand the traditional and limited marketing role of the Internet for your business without exceeding your budget limitations.

62. To increase sales and improve service, businesses should offer interactive capabilities for customers to place orders, make inquiries, request bids, and download product catalogs and service manuals. Many businesses now use the Internet to allow patients and clients to book or change their own appointments. It can be a very useful tool to help reduce lost revenue by sending an email or text message to confirm scheduled appointments. Online customer access need not be a cost prohibitive luxury viable only for "big box" retailers and national catalog companies. Multiple studies confirm it is a necessity for many types of small businesses. For example:

- In an October 18, 2010 article titled *A Cheery Holiday Forecast,* Thad Rueter of the *Internet Retailer* reported on the results of a survey by The National Retail Federation. The survey found 44% of consumers ages 18 and above planned to shop online during the 2010 Christmas season. Of consumers who earned at least $50,000, 55% would shop online. Perhaps more telling of emerging trends, 27% of U.S. consumers who own a smartphone were expected to use it to research and buy products.

- An article titled *8 Ways Fullservice Operators Can Build Sales* was published by the National Restaurant Association in their *2010 Restaurant Industry Outlook Forecast.* It reported that 41% of consumers surveyed said they choose new restaurants because of e-mail promotions. Close to 30% said they would likely opt to receive e-mail notification of daily specials. Another 56% visit restaurant websites, 54% view restaurant menus, 54% use the Internet to learn about restaurants they have not patronized while 25% have made reservations online.

63. If your business uses or is considering using gift cards, look at Panera Bread and McAlister's Deli websites. Both offer the ability to sell, recharge and check card balances online, a real customer convenience. Providing printable coupons online is an even easier customer benefit you can offer.

Email Marketing and Surveys:

64. Offer an incentive to prospects willing to opt-in or join your mailing list. We have all jotted down invalid information to escape the clutches of a pushy sales person. Therefore, do not hand out coupons or gifts on the spot; mail or email them. That way invalid data costs nothing.

65. Once you have established a customer and prospect database, it is time to consider an email marketing campaign through a vendor like:

- BenchmarkEmail

- Campaigner

- ConstantContact

- iContact

- MailChimp

- Pinpointe

- VerticalResponse

These low-cost (several are free depending on the size of your mailing list and the number of monthly emails) services allow you to download and manage email lists, and to create professional looking newsletters and other documents. They give recipients the ability to click through to your website for more information, and to forward emails to others. If they like what they see, their network then has the opportunity to opt-in to your mailing list. Email marketing services also offer the ability to promote, manage and even collect registration fees for event-based marketing ideas as discussed in Chapters 6 and 12 of this book. Keep the following points in mind in your analysis and planning process:

- **Structure email campaigns so you can track actual sales and new leads.** There are several ways to accomplish this. One is to offer unique promotions or promotional codes in each communication channel. Another is to require customers to print the email promotion and present it in person to redeem it.

- Prices for email marketing services vary. They can be based on fixed monthly fees, sliding scales depending on the size of your mailing list, or a fixed charge per email. Several vendors offer limited free trials. Shop around and speak with your network contacts to find the one that best fits your needs and budget.

- Perhaps most importantly, email marketing vendors help ensure compliance with the Federal Trade Commission's *Controlling the Assault of Non-Solicited Pornography and Marketing Act* (CAN-SPAM) of 2003. This is the federal standard for commercial email.

Consider the following ideas when developing your email-marketing plan.

66. Email marketing commands far more attention if it includes special offers, coupons or discounts. For example, there is a colorful gourmet restaurant near my home. It has been featured on the Food Network's television show *Diners, Drive-ins and Dives* with Guy Fieri. Friends and customers are treated to a coupon for a free serving of the restaurant's signature dessert when they opt-in to the mailing list. They then receive a monthly newsletter that promotes new menu items, shares recipes, and so on. It always includes a coupon for a free dessert, 10% off an entree or a similar enticement. Their website and newsletters promote their Facebook page, Twitter account, blog and numerous YouTube videos. To see this outstanding example of an integrated Internet and social media marketing campaign, visit www.chefpointcafe.org. While I cannot comment on its financial success, I will tell you if you happen to be near Watauga, Texas around mealtime, stop in. However, plan on waiting in a long line.

- Study emails you receive and think about what makes them appealing or ineffective. **It is always cheaper to learn from someone else's mistakes than to make them yourself!**

67. Online surveys are such a flexible and valuable marketing tool that it is difficult to structure an argument not to conduct them on a regular basis. Most

of the vendors listed in Idea #65 offer survey capabilities, as do a myriad of other Internet vendors (see www.SurveyMonkey.com as an example). Several of the social media platforms discussed in Chapter 7 also offer free tools for simple surveys. Begin to explore these options by Goggling "Twitter survey tools." Given the wide variety of competing vendors, there is probably no reason to spend more than $300 a year for even the largest of survey programs.

Surveys can offer feedback from current and former customers, or an entire market. They can also provide market intelligence on your competition and industry. Surveys monitor customer perceptions of your entire value proposition (see Appendix I), namely your products, services and prices. They can also help uncover aspects of your value proposition that customers are unaware of, or perhaps undervalue relative to your costs.

While a complete outline of a survey program is well beyond the intended scope of this book, here are a few quick points you should keep in mind:

- Begin your survey with a clearly defined plan. What do you hope to learn, what questions will help you gather the information necessary to achieve your goals, and what actions will you take because of the information gathered?

- Make questions clear, precise and short. Each should address only one area or piece of information. For example, responses may be ambiguous if participants are asked about price and service in the same question.

- Close-ended questions (where the respondent selects from a limited number of specified answers) are easier to analyze. Open-ended questions provide more qualitative information. Consider a combination of both types of questions.

- Being constantly patted on the back accomplishes little, other than eventually wearing out the fabric on your shoulder. In business, it is far more valuable to receive an honest assessment of what you are doing wrong. Therefore, be willing to accept and act on the results of your survey, warts and all. Nevertheless, a press release may be in order if a favorable outcome justifies it.

- Ask how likely the respondent is to do business with you again and how likely they are to recommend you to someone else. If either answer is no, determine why.

- Construct surveys so they take no more than 10 minutes to complete.

- Offer an incentive (like a 20% coupon) for those who give you the 10 minutes.

- If you decide to incorporate the U.S. Postal Service to survey customers without Internet access, include a postage-paid return envelope. Your response percentage will be abysmal without one.

Here are a few final points that apply to your evaluation and implementation of both email marketing and survey campaigns:

- You will be surprised how few people open your email. ConstantContact tracks "open rates" by about 30 industry categories. Marketing and PR firms (who should be able to achieve stellar results) are 13%. The highest category is only 27%. It is a numbers game, so do not get discouraged. **Above all, do not confuse activity with results in your accountability evaluation.** A 100% open rate is worthless unless it generates sales, develops new leads or gathers useful marketing data.

- Two other valuable statistics are your bounce rate (percentage of undeliverable emails) and your clickthrough rate (percentage of recipients who visit your website from the email link). The first shows how current and accurate your email lists are. The second provides a measure of the effectiveness of your online campaign. Compare both rates to industry averages as published by ConstantContact or one of the other vendors.

- Consider the typical schedule and workload of your intended audience. Emails and surveys sent to accountants on April 14 or to retailers the week before Christmas are not going to achieve acceptable response rates.

- Ralph Waldo Emerson said, "All life is an experiment. The more experiments you make the better." Apply his philosophy by scheduling mailings on different days of the week and different times of the day. Never schedule a mailing immediately before or after a holiday. It will be deleted in the rush to leave early or buried in an avalanche of emails that piled up over the long weekend.

- Also, experiment with the frequency of distributions. Depending on how you use email, you may decide to do weekly or monthly mailings. Get into a regular routine. Victoria's Secret sends daily emails. My wife finds this excessive, presumptuous and annoying. I might be forced to unsubscribe if they do not slow down. Then again, maybe not. It is all about content.

- Many recipients make snap decisions whether to open or delete an email based solely on its subject line. Choose something inviting that suggests a reason to read it. As previously mentioned, titles in the form of questions, "how to" advice, self-help tips or lists are usually effective.

- Again, always have someone proofread every communication before issuing it.

Web-based Sales Platforms:

68. There is nothing new or cutting edge about suggesting eBay as a sales platform. The world's most popular online auction website has been around since late 1995 when founder Pierre Omidyar sold a broken laser pointer for $14.83. In all fairness, he later sold a Gulfstream jet for $4.9 million. According to eBay's website, gross merchandise volume for 2009 approached $60 billion thanks to 90 million users and numerous specialty websites. Retailers can use individual listings or eBay stores. They can offer products using traditional auctions, fixed prices or fixed prices with best-offer options.

    To be sure, eBay has its detractors. However, depending on the nature of your products and operations, there may be a place for eBay in your marketing strategy.

    - Analyze and define your eBay marketing strategy through a little homework and some low-cost experimentation. Why not list a few items and see what happens?

    - If eBay becomes a significant part of your marketing efforts, consider the impact of your Internet pricing strategy on existing "brick and mortar" sales. You will have to balance the added cost of shipping against the marketing risk of under-pricing online products relative to what customers are charged in your physical location.

69. National websites that distribute coupons and advertise specials are interesting and growing promotional vehicles. Perhaps the best know of these so-called "deal of the day" enterprises is Groupon. It was the subject of an August 30, 2010 Forbes Magazine article called *Meet the Fastest Growing Company Ever* by Christopher Steiner. Its name is a play on the words "group" and "coupon," a misnomer since customers purchase discounted vouchers, not coupons. If your specified minimum number of customers is achieved, you are paid immediately. It costs nothing unless the offer is completed.

Groupon's compensation is a healthy portion of the offering proceeds, plus credit card fees. Customer discounts of at least 50% seem to be the norm. Groupon is therefore a viable platform to distribute gift cards and to introduce customers to high margin products or services, especially where additional full-price sales are anticipated during the initial or repeat sales.

• The most obvious risk of incorporating Groupon into your marketing plan is attracting customers who will only buy at a substantial discount. If your Groupon pricing strategy is contingent on support from full-price repeat sales, this venue could become a textbook example of a strategy that increases sales while decreasing net income. Monitor results closely and be prepared to run away if necessary.

- Another possible concern is that your promotion will be announced as part of a daily email distribution scheduled by Groupon; you have no control over its timing.

- Finally, it is possible to become a victim of your own success with Groupon if you do not place an upper limit on how many discount vouchers you are willing to sell. This can happen in at least two ways. First, if your offer is attractive enough, placing limits on it (experiment as you would with any new promotion) will avoid the risk of having more customers than you can accommodate. A line of unhappy customer wannbes standing outside your store with Groupon vouchers in hand is not good public relations. Secondly, you are likely to lose money on every Groupon sale. For example, a $100 gift card offered for $50 will only generate about $23 in your pocket. Further assume the cost of providing that $100 of goods or service is $80. You will therefore lose about $57 on every Groupon voucher. **Know your numbers and factor the expected gross loss into your marketing budget.**

70. If the economics or mechanics of Groupon simply do not work for your business, you are not alone. However, you may have cost effective alternatives readily available. Groupon is quickly gaining new competition. An article in the April 25, 2011 edition of *Forbes Focus* by Brendan Coffey estimated Groupon has 425 "me-too" competitors, and suggested that future competition may include Facebook and Google.

Groupon rejected a $6 billion buy-out offer from Google in December of 2010.

While I have not evaluated specific vendors, here are several options you may wish to explore on your own.

- Some cities and regions are creating websites to distribute coupons and advertise specials to promote local businesses, and typically at a lower net cost than the big-name national sites. I was pleased to see several such sites advertise on television during a visit to the Central Coast region of California. As an example, look at www.slocoupons.com. It promotes commerce in San Luis Obispo County. Search the Internet and ask your network contacts for comparable programs in your area.

- Socialdish.com is scheduled to launch in March 2011, so its ultimate success has yet to be determined as of this writing. However, what makes it worth watching is that it is structured as a multilevel marketing program. It will distribute 30% of its fees through 10 levels of "downlines" as people recruit their friends and family. The limited information available at this time indicates Socialdish's charges to advertisers will be less than Groupon.

- LivingSocial.com is another "deal-of-the-day" type competitor to Groupon. This company was partially financed by the online retail juggernaut Amazon.

Numerous state, local and national Internet websites allow you to promote your services or locate potential clients at little or no cost. Some will subject you to international competition, and several have experienced their share of criticism and controversy. Terms and conditions vary; shop around and investigate to find websites appropriate for your business.

New websites pop up regularly. Here are a few to get you started.

71. Elance.com provides an online marketplace for consultants and others to search for assignments, submit bids and negotiate contracts. The largest categories are information technology and marketing, including web development, programming and search engine optimization. Elance assesses their fee on payments by businesses to consultants.

72. Craigslist is a centralized network of online communities featuring free classified advertisements with sections devoted to sale items and services. According to the Factsheet on their website, Craigslist operates through 700 local websites in 70 countries. It claims 50 million users in the U.S. alone. Craigslist experiences over 20 billion page views per month, making it the seventh largest site worldwide for English language page views.

73. Fiverr.com offers products and services for $5, of which the website keeps $1. Its challenges and limitations are immediately apparent, starting with whether you want

to offer anything for five bucks! You will be surprised at the offerings. Two actual examples are, "I will teach you how to make your hands a flute for $5" and "I will take a photo of myself holding a logo of any website, company, etc. for $5." Therefore, you should carefully consider whether being in the same crowd would cheapen your brand. For that reason alone, it may not be appropriate. However, if you are willing to offer virtually free products or services to gain new customers, it merits consideration.

74. OLX hosts free user-generated classified ads for urban communities around the world and provides discussion forums for various topics. It gained prominence upon announcing a partnership with Friendster, a social networking website.

75. Guru.com is also a freelance marketplace that allows companies to find consultants for contract work in 220 different fields. Guru's website reports over 1 million registered members and over 8,000 projects posted per month. Be aware that if the service you are marketing can be delivered remotely, competition from English-speaking competitors in developing countries in Asia and elsewhere will likely exert strong downward pressure on your price expectations. That is why I no longer advertise on Guru.com.

76. Finally, several large online business directory listings are available free of charge and can be set up within minutes. These directories provide a valuable tool to enable business owners to manage and enhance their

Internet presence. For that reason, they are especially important for companies who do not have their own website. These sites promote connection through online searches by potential customers. Companies can post extensive information. Listings typically include business categories, web addresses, locations, hours, payment options and detailed product and service descriptions. They may allow you to upload photos, and some offer coupon and promotional capabilities. Many allow customers to post reviews. Some of the larger directories are:

- Google Places

- Bing Local

- Yahoo Local

- Hotfrog

All are free, often with upgraded services available for a fee. Google Places offers the ability to post real-time updates. It also provides a dashboard to track how many times people found your business and what keywords they used to find it.

Here is a closing thought for this chapter on *Internet Marketing Basics*. Michael Dylan is an entrepreneur and business enthusiast. He summarized the ultimate challenge of Internet marketing this way: "In real-world shopping, you can look your customers right in the eye, chat with them and thus understand what they want, or guide them to a certain item. But with so much online business, we need to establish good customer relations in cyber-space, including ways to find out what the customer needs and what they really value in your business."

I encourage you to remember Mr. Dylan's comment as you develop and implement your Internet marketing strategies.

Chapter 9

COUPONS, DISCOUNTS & GIFT CERTIFICATES

When was the last time you clipped a 10-cent coupon from a newspaper? It was probably between when you last listened to music on an  eight-track tape player and when you last played Space Invaders on your Atari 2600. I ask that tongue-in-cheek question to introduce three important rules.

Rule #1: Coupons, discounts and gift certificates must be large enough to grab customers' attention and motivate them to take advantage of your offer. The last time 10 cents bought a first-class postage stamp was 1975. On the other hand, try to offer coupons and discounts that allow room for a small gross profit. A 30%-off coupon still generates 70% of the ticketed price. It will increase your bottom line if your gross margin is say 35%. Likewise, a $50 coupon for your tax services will command attention. However, if the average tax return costs $175, it will still generate $125 in sales. **A small businessperson can never have too much knowledge about their cost structure when designing profitable promotions.**

Rule #2: To be effective, your target market must be aware of the promotion. For example, a February 2009 Pew Research Center report said only 27% of Americans born after 1976 read a newspaper the previous day. If the under-35 demographic is your target audience and you only advertise in printed newspapers, the majority of your market will never see your ads. You must communicate your message in media where customers can see it. Do not overlook customers who research vendors and place orders through websites, text messages or with smartphones. Use as many platforms as possible to communicate your promotions.

Rule #3: Coupons must get into the hands of customers who will redeem them. Who is more likely to perceive value and take advantage of your promotions than an existing, satisfied customer? I am always impressed when I study the coupons on the back of grocery receipts. They are not only 15% off anything in the store, nor are they all identical to customers in front or behind me in the checkout line. Some are unique to me and targeted to specific products. The store's information system is able to recall individual buying habits and offer incentives on items similar or complementary to recent purchases. For example, if I buy razor blades today, next week's coupons might include a free can of shaving cream. Unfortunately, small businesses are unlikely to have the system capabilities to support promotions requiring this level of sophistication. Rule #3 still applies!

Experiment with coupons, discounts and gift certificates using the following low-cost ideas.

77. You may not be able to track individual buying habits. However, you should obviously get to know something

about every regular customer. For example, there is no point offering a cat food coupon to a dog owner. Knowing basic, observable information like approximate age, gender, marital status, date of last purchase, average purchase and so on will begin to accumulate customer profiles to tailor promotions to their specific wants and needs. Your eyes and ears, and those of your employees, are probably the most useful tools in this fact gathering process.

- You do not need an expensive information system to accumulate and analyze your data. A simple database program like Microsoft Access or even Excel will help get you started.

- Customer profiles also provide valuable accountability input. It is almost inevitable that your business will have some unprofitable customers. They are too small, buy too infrequently, are too service intensive, slow in paying, or only buy products on sale. Yet, their customer support may cost as much as for profitable customers. Increase your bottom line by re-pricing or dropping these customers as your profiling efforts identify them.

78. Program cash registers to print generic promotions on the back or bottom of sales receipts. Everyone will get the same offer, but at least the coupon is in your customer's possession. That is a step in the right direction!

79. Another alternative is to simply put a stamp or sticker on receipts and invoices, or just drop a flyer in the customer's bag at checkout. Starbucks sometimes stamps morning receipts for afternoon discounts on iced coffee, driving traffic to the slowest part of their day. Either tactic gives you the ability to modify promotions quickly and at minimal cost. The point is you are getting coupons into the hands of customers who have already demonstrated a willingness to do business with you.

80. Perhaps the only thing more frustrating than failing to get coupons into your customers' hands is when competitors succeed in reaching the same audience. No problem! Let your competitors do the heavy (and expensive) lifting and simply accept their coupons. It is an often-overlooked fact that many of the nation's top retailers do exactly that. Although not all seem to advertise their policy, Target, Walmart, PetSmart, Winn Dixie, CVS, Home Depot, Staples and many others accept competitor coupons with certain restrictions.

- Research what competitors and other businesses in your area are doing.

- Imposing reasonable restrictions is prudent as you measure the financial impact of this strategy. Examples would be matching competitor coupons only up to 20% or limiting them to $25 off.

- Educate your customers and promote your new policy. It will generate additional sales.

81. Supermarkets have long championed weekly specials. So should you. There is no reason why you cannot promote more than one item at a time, or offer product specific and generic promotions on the same advertisement or flyer. Experiment with different combinations, gauging consumer preferences and buying habits in the process. It is a great way to introduce new products and encourage sales of slow moving items.

82. Discount end of season, discontinued or clearance items, below cost if necessary. That way you avoid additional expenses like restocking and insurance, and minimize the risk of damage or theft during storage. If customers ordinarily buy multiples of seasonal or slow moving products, you can move inventory with a 2-for-1 or a buy-one-get-one free (BOGO) sale as it is called in retail. If not, give the items away with another purchase. Another marketing wrinkle might be disposing of these items through eBay. Use the cash you generate to invest in new products.

Generating Repeat Sales:

The late William Edwards Deming, an American author, lecturer, and consultant wrote about an important marketing phenomenon. He said, "Profit in business comes from repeat customers, customers that boast about your project or service, and that bring friends with them." Mr. Deming's comment suggests an important question. **If repeat customers are so valuable, what are you doing to turn first-time customers into repeat buyers?**

83. Car salespeople know a secret about repeat customers. They do not negotiate as hard as first-time buyers do. Likewise, every insurance agent knows longtime policyholders experience fewer losses. Existing customers in any business, presumably happy with its products and service, are more likely to make referrals to friends and family.

Let me share a specific example of how one nearby luxury day spa applies this principle. First, new customers are mailed discounts for spa services they have not yet purchased. If they forget the coupons on their next visit, no problem. The spa tracks unused discounts for them. Customers separately receive discount cards for friends and family, each inscribed with their name. This adds a personal touch and allows the spa to track referrals. Finally, first-timers are added to the spa's 3,000 plus mailing list to receive future promotions. Any bets on whether the customer will receive a card and a promotion on their next birthday?

The lesson here is merely to remember the earlier quote by Mary Kay Ash. Recognize the invisible sign around first-time customers' necks. Make them feel important, or they will not give you a second chance.

84. Here is another example of how to generate repeat sales with coupons and discounts. Follow up recent sales with a personalized note thanking customers for their business. Include in the note a special limited-time offer for a related item. For example, if they recently bought a pair of shoes, offer 25% off a matching purse

or belt. Include an expiration date to create a sense of urgency.

85. Another way to retain customers and encourage repeat sales is to incorporate coupons, discounts or gift certificates as the basis of a preferred customer or loyalty program. Everyone is familiar with the example of preferred diner cards where every 10th meal is free.

- Your preferred customer program must be generous enough that customers perceive value in it, yet not so generous that you have no hope of eventually making a profit.

- Promote your preferred customer program through email, social media and all other communication tools at your disposal. Most importantly, do not overlook your own workforce. Properly trained and incentivized cashiers, sales people and other employees with direct customer interaction will probably recruit more members for your loyalty program than all other sources combined.

- Some stores and national chains charge a fee for preferred customer discount programs. Aside from my reluctance to spend money for something other than actual products or services, I invariably forget to use the program when I make a purchase. I am never happy when I realize I lost an opportunity to save money. On the few occasions where I have been talked into signing up, I rarely renew the program beyond the initial year. A better alternative to charging a fee may be to offer free membership for those who meet reasonable qualification requirements. Examples would be a minimum total purchase over the previous 12 months, or a single large order over a specified amount. This method will provide an additional opportunity to touch customers by communicating their good fortune at having achieved your elite preferred customer status.

86. **Maintaining existing customer relationships is even more critical to your marketing success than turning first-time customers into repeat buyers.** Trying to win back former customers is therefore a logical and usually cost effective strategy. Here is what one store did to lure me back.

Over the last few years, 20% of my clothing purchases have been from one store. I have used $595 of their preferred customer gift certificates. However, I had not made a purchase in a year. The store knows my past buying habits. What they do not know is they are still my favorite men's store. I just had not spent much on clothes recently. Therefore, it came as no surprise when I received a promotion for $25 off my next purchase and extra points in their preferred customer program. I suddenly realized I could use a few new shirts.

- A little data mining of your sales records will identify customers who have not made recent purchases. Send them a survey to determine what changed their buying habits, or pick up the phone and ask them.

- Alternatively, send them a coupon and see if they respond.

87. Allow me to expand on the previous ideas of how to maintain existing customer relationships. America has been a country on the move ever since it was founded by people who all crossed an ocean to get here. The U.S. Census Bureau reports that the national mover rate was 12.5% in 2009. According to their *Geographical Mobility: 2009* study, 37.1 million people changed residences in the U.S. that year. Of those, 67.3% stayed within the same county, 17.2% moved to a different county in the same state, 12.6% moved to a different state, and 2.9% moved to the U.S. from abroad.

Furthermore, the National Association of Realtors reported in January 2011 that the previous month's existing home sales (including single-family, townhomes, condominiums and co-ops) was a seasonally adjusted annual rate of 5.9 million. Experts tell us that the demographics of people moving, buying and selling houses are heavily influenced by age, occupation and income levels. The young, professionals and high-income earners are among the most likely candidates.

These statistics are troubling if you provide landscaping, pest control, cleaning, HVAC maintenance or a host of other home-based or recurring services. It does not require much data extrapolation to see that if you lose 10% or 12% of your customers every year to moves (possibly more if your market is concentrated in young, high-income professionals) you will soon be in big trouble. Even if you are able to replace customers who migrate outside of your service area, consulting firm Lee Resources International, Inc. reports that attracting a new customer costs five times as much as keeping an existing one.

- Hanging on to your existing customer base with coupons, discounts and gift certificates is always more cost effective. Offer movers a meaningful incentive to transfer your services to their new home. A free month, a 10% discount on your standard rates or a similar promotion will prove cheaper and have a higher success rate in maintaining your customer base than finding new customers.

- The mirror image of this idea is to offer customers who are moving an incentive to provide a referral to the new homeowner. However, several potential issues make it less likely to generate sales. First, it does not apply to customers living in non-owner occupied homes such as apartment complexes. Furthermore, assuming their home has already sold, your old customers probably do not know the new owners. Finally, homeowners will not be motivated by additional discounts off your services if they are moving out of the area. Offer the original homeowner a $25 gift card from a national restaurant chain or retailer if the new homeowner becomes your customer because of their referral.

- Alternatively, send the new homeowner a promotional offer touting the fact that you are familiar with their home and neighborhood since you provided service for the previous owner.

- Finally, Welcome Wagon's website lists ample reasons to target new homeowners and tenants, even if you did not provide services to the previous occupant. They point out that new homeowners spend 20 times more than established residents. That includes $102 billion on move-related products. Most importantly, they have no existing buying loyalties in their new community, and are seeking information about products and services they will need. Once again, the need to educate the consumer presents a key marketing and growth opportunity for the observant businessperson.

Here are a few closing thoughts on this critical marketing topic of using coupons, discounts and gift certificates as effective marketing tools:

A. **Design your promotion to accomplish specific marketing goals.** If you recently introduced a new product line, offer 20% off those items. If your goal is to increase the average sale per customer, offer $10 off purchases of $50 or more. If you simply want to encourage repeat business, offer a free product most customers are likely to use. Supermarkets often use staples like milk or gasoline for their give-away promotions.

B. Do not diminish the value of a promotion by placing unreasonable restrictions on it. Unless targeted to a specific customer, allow coupons and gift certificates to be freely transferable and have reasonable expiration dates. Customer purchased gift certificates should never expire. Many merchants honor promotions for a few days after expiration as a gesture of goodwill. As Marshall Field said, "That is the one and only asset that competition cannot undersell or destroy." Moreover, a sale is a sale. If it brings a new customer into your business a week late, where is the harm?

C. The "fine print" on some purchased gift certificate and card programs discloses a monthly inactivity fee. It is far too common for vendors to reduce outstanding balances by 1% or 2% per month if not used. In essence, they charge customers a fee for making them an interest-free loan. Be aware that consumers may perceive this practice as inappropriate. It is certainly shortsighted. Do not risk long-term customer relationships for the sake of inconsequential short-term gains.

D. Finally, depending on how customer purchased gift certificate and card programs are structured and the states in which they were sold, merchants may be required to eventually escheat (turn over to the state) any balance that customers fail to redeem. Potential issuers should consult their state treasurer's office or the National Association of Unclaimed Property Administrators. Again, meeting the reporting requirements of escheat laws will strain the limits of the average small business accounting system.

Chapter 10

BEING A GOOD CORPORATE CITIZEN

Today, more than any time in recent memory, there are countless deserving charities and community groups that will benefit greatly from any support or assistance your business can provide.

Since these organizations are often managed by what I call "centers of influence" (local clergy, business leaders and other prominent members of the community), your involvement will communicate your value proposition to a wide audience of influential people with attractive demographics. Keep in mind that if your primary motive is merely a selfish desire to profit off the name of a charity it can cause far more harm than benefit, as it should.

Consider the following ideas and suggestions.

88. Charitable support does not have to mean cash out of your pocket. It also includes allowing groups to post notices of upcoming fundraisers in your front window, using your parking lot for car washes and selling cookies on your sidewalk. Most antique car shows I participate in are charity fundraisers sponsored by local restaurants. Their support does not go unnoticed or

unrewarded. Few advertisements can attract more spontaneous prospects than a few rows of muscle cars parked in plain view of a busy thoroughfare. I have often witnessed car enthusiasts quickly fill restaurant parking lots to overflowing on slow Sunday afternoons. Furthermore, a coupon for a free appetizer, and the hot Texas sun, are all the encouragement most car owners need to spend a few dollars on cold beverages. I discovered my favorite BBQ restaurant while attending a car show, and won a "Top 20" award in the bargain.

89. Here is another example of charitable support that does not have to require any cash. **Do something tangible and visible to help your community.** Adopt a street, sponsor food drives or fundraisers, clothing collections and so on. I was invited to a seminar held 10 days before Thanksgiving. The cost of admission was a donation of canned goods to a local food bank, not a bad price for two hours of CPE!

- Encourage (but do not require) employee involvement with the charity. You will build camaraderie and create a greater sense of community in the process. It will also allow employees to grow and expand their business networks.

- Recognize and reward contributors and supporters; you never know where it will lead. I first became aware of a vital community need when my employer offered blood donors the day off. I have since received American Red Cross "gallon pins" and continue to be a donor 25 years later. I have also enjoyed an extra week or so of vacation.

90. You can gain access to a broad new market by simply setting up a table at charity and community events. My wife manages a retail store. She sponsors fashion shows and similar affairs for local women's clubs and senior activity centers. The organizations' members usually serve as models. Not surprisingly, they often buy the outfits they model.

   • A small donation or commission on sales may convince an organization to become your defacto marketing partner if they have not done so in the past.

91. **Volunteer at organizations that serve your target market or that have some logical connection to your business.** For example, a youth league is a natural fit for a sporting goods store. A network associate of mine supports a blood bank next door to his store. Supporters are personally invited over to pick up a gender-specific gift bag after they donate blood. My last donation netted an attractive Swiss Army Knife.

   • Look for roles within the charity that offer maximum exposure to members. Staffing the sign-in desk or serving as a greeter are great ways to meet people. I once volunteered as a greeter for a regional senior citizen forum. I met one of my County Commissioners and a nationally recognized author and columnist for the largest newspaper in the area. I am now a Facebook friend with both men.

- Any role that allows you to communicate your skill and expertise is valuable.

92. Offer your product or service to local charities. A cleaning service I know offers free housecleaning to cancer patients. You can stretch your generosity and serve a wider audience by having the charity supply the labor while you provide the technical knowledge, supplies and so on. A word of caution is appropriate:

- It is fine to have a volunteer operate a vacuum cleaner. Do not let them near expensive or dangerous equipment, even if they possess the necessary skills and experience to operate it. Avoid possible liability issues by not allowing volunteers to operate your company vehicles and insured equipment.

93. Donating gift certificates or baskets filled with your products to charity auctions is a great way to increase visibility within your community. Come to think of it, what is to stop you from supporting charities in neighboring communities where you also draw customers?

94. Consider allocating a portion of your marketing budget to support local charities. Make a promotional flyer (you already have all the tools you need on your PC) and hire a youth group to distribute it in

neighborhoods, shopping center parking lots, sporting events and community events. Take out ads in community group bulletins and newsletters. You can also offer special discounts to their members. I once attended a church that received a small contribution from a local grocery store for all cash register receipts collected from church members. The promotion was prominently mentioned in the church bulletin every Sunday.

95. Homeowners associations are not charitable entities. However, I include them in this chapter because they are non-profit organizations. HOAs have the added advantage of easily observable and homogeneous demographics. Do not overlook them when offering targeted special discounts and similar promotions. They may also welcome your sponsorship of their newsletters and neighborhood events.

96. Because of the close physical proximity of prospects, homeowners associations with whom you have established a marketing relationship are an ideal setting in which to experiment with a door hanger campaign. You can print flyers on your computer, order door hangers from any print shop or online, or order the paper stock and print them yourself. Think about hiring your favorite charity youth group to distribute them for you.

Finally, balancing the needs of your business with the needs of the communities it serves is always difficult. John Mackey is the CEO and cofounder of Whole Foods Market, and Ernst & Young's 2003 Entrepreneur of the Year. He addressed this delicate balance: "I think one of the most misunderstood things about business in America is that people are either doing things for altruistic reasons or they are greedy and selfish, just after profit. That type of dichotomy portrays a false image of business. The whole idea is to do both."

In other words, being a good corporate citizen means serving your community as you grow your business, two completely compatible and praise-worthy goals.

Chapter 11

REDUCE RISK TO INCREASE SALES

A basic human characteristic has the potential to influence any sale. **Customers are adverse to risk and uncertainty!** Remove the risk (real or perceived) of doing business with you, and your closing rates will improve. Otherwise, you are telling prospects to roll the dice and "take  a chance on me." While that made for a popular Abba song, as a marketing strategy, it has some obvious flaws.

These uncertainties instill a level of customer distrust. Starbucks CEO Howard Schultz explained the reason for this distrust. "In the 1960s, if you introduced a new product to America, 90% of the people who viewed it for the first time believed in the corporate promise. Forty years later, if you performed the same exercise less than 10% of the public believed it was true. The fracturing of trust is based on the fact that the consumer has been let down."

Your challenge is to overcome distrust and risk aversion. Here are seven ways to help you meet that challenge.

97. Customers want to know approximately how much they should expect to spend in advance, without having to keep an anxious eye on the clock. This is often an issue for lawyers, CPAs and other highly compensated

professionals who generally charge hourly rates. If this situation applies to your business, structure an introductory offer. For example, as an attorney with a billing rate of $250 per hour, you might offer to incorporate a new business, obtain all required permits and tax identification numbers and organize their corporate records for $499 including an initial consultation. If the project can be completed within two hours, you earned your standard rate. If not, the introductory offer still works if you provide subsequent services using your regular fee schedule. You may also land full-price referrals because of your introductory offer.

- As you complete assignments, you will likely find ways to reduce time and costs, lowering your breakeven point in the process.

- The introductory price is independent of who performs the work. You can further reduce your costs if you can delegate portions of the assignment to your staff or outsource to lower-cost vendors.

98. There is probably no law that says you must bill clients the same way competing vendors do. Another way to reduce customers' risk perceptions is therefore to just break whatever pricing model exists in your business and pull ahead of the pack! A timely example is the U.S. Postal Service's priority shipping program. Using the slogan, "If it fits, it ships," they charge by package size while the competition charges by weight. This has the obvious advantage of allowing customers to determine

the required package size and cost without having to guess at its weight. The Postal Service also offers free packages, which can be ordered online.

If your competitors charge by the hour, offer fixed fees. If competitors require an annual contract, offer customers month-to-month services. Consider the following points when evaluating this idea:

- The strategy may be especially effective while initially establishing a revenue base to cover fixed costs like rent and overhead. This is another example of why it is always important to understand your numbers.

- You are not locked into the same pricing methodology after your business is established. You can also re-price services as necessary in subsequent years, as long as you do not give the appearance of discriminating against returning customers in favor of new ones.

- As with the previous suggestion, you will likely learn efficiencies and improve your estimating skills. Adjust your prices accordingly.

99. We have all ventured out of our culinary shell from time to time and took a risk by ordering a new entree or dessert, only to discover we hated it. Ice cream shops have found a cheap yet completely effective way of eliminating this risk. They offer free samples on tiny plastic spoons. I am told the sample (including the

spoon) costs less than two cents. Supermarkets hand out free food samples in little plastic cups. Wine tastings accomplish the same objective. Free samples, or alternatively a free trial period, may be the best way to encourage customers to try new products or services without the fear of having to pay for something that does not meet their needs or tastes.

100. My next suggestion under the topic of reducing risk to increase sales is an extension of the previous one. It is admittedly controversial. The idea is to provide free service in the hope of gaining new customers for full-price services. However, what you are giving away is neither the "2-cent sample" variety of Idea #99, nor the deluxe version of your service. It is somewhere in-between, probably closer to the former than the latter. Your free offering should be either a limited version of your primary service, or a less expensive auxiliary service.

- For example, if you are a personal wealth manager, offer a free analysis of a prospect's retirement investments. That is an important part of your main service. Your hope is obviously that some prospects will be so impressed with your knowledge and advice (or so unhappy with their current manager) that they will retain you to manage their portfolio. Other examples of providing a free service include a carpet cleaner who offers to clean one room free of charge, or an alarm company conducting a free home security analysis.

- Jewelry stores illustrate an example of attracting customers with auxiliary services. They often provide free ring cleanings or replacement batteries for watches. With the highest gross profit margins in retail, very few prospects have to make additional full-price purchases in order to make the free service a successful strategy.

Satisfaction Guarantees:

101. Customer risk perceptions include concerns that your product or service might not perform as promised. **To overcome this concern, and to be truly distinctive, customer service must include clearly defined after-sale policies and procedures.** L.L.Bean, named number 1 in customer service for 2008 by *Business Week*, pioneered the "lifetime satisfaction guarantee" 100 years ago. Sears has offered a similar lifetime warranty on their popular Craftsman tool line since its introduction in 1927. Over 80 years later, a March 2009 announcement on the MySearsCommunity.com website said, "Our Craftsman Hand Tool Lifetime Warranty is one of the most important competitive advantages we have in the market."

Will some customers take advantage of a generous return policy? Without question. However, occasionally dealing with unhappy and even unreasonable customers is an unavoidable cost of doing business. A lifetime "no-questions-asked" return policy is probably not necessary. However, the nature of your product or service and the terms offered by competitors may require a policy that includes repairs, refunds or store credit for a reasonable period following the sale.

- Once again, accountability is a key element of success. **You must be able to track the cost of returns and refunds, and have at least an intuitive gauge of their impact on customer satisfaction levels versus the cost of lost business.** The White House Office of Consumer Affairs reports that the average dissatisfied consumer can be expected to tell between 9 and 15 people about their experience. Approximately 13% will actually tell more than 20 people. Compare those prospects to the results of a survey by Lee Resources. They found that 70% of complaining customers would do business with you again if you resolve the complaint in their favor. Fully 95% will do business with you again if you resolve the complaint immediately.

102. The previous idea applies to the sale of products more than to services. With that said, a self-described marketing expert once insisted I needed to offer a "100% money-back guarantee" to win new clients. It gets worse! He also suggested I guarantee savings of at least 10 times my fee. I had two major issues with the suggestion. First, in a profession where it was actually illegal to advertise only a few years ago, it sounded too much like an old-fashioned "snake oil" marketing approach. Secondly, all I do is counsel and advise clients. The value of my advice is ultimately dependent on their success in implementing recommendations in a

timely fashion. I cannot guarantee the actions of others. Neither can you!

With that said, the concept of a money-back guarantee might have value to service providers within some narrowly defined parameters. Carefully consider the following matters:

- At the risk of sounding like a cynic, get paid up front. Clients will be less likely to take advantage of your guarantee if they have to look you in the eye and lie about their dissatisfaction while asking for a refund.

- Place clear and reasonable boundaries on what customers must do to qualify for a refund. Assume for example that I promise to develop your website and have it running within 60 days. That commitment must be contingent upon you providing a list of items like graphics and content, and on your timely approval of my work at various stages of completion. If your failure to perform those obligations is the primary cause of me missing the deadline, forget the money-back guarantee.

- Consider offering a money-back guarantee on only part of your services. For example, weight loss centers advertise you will lose 20 pounds in 10 weeks for $20, or you get your money back. Since these centers cannot guarantee customers will follow the program, they cannot guarantee anyone will lose weight. They do not seem to fret much over that minor annoyance. Part of the weight loss program is that you eat their food for the entire 10 weeks. That will cost another $75 or more a week. No one can reasonably expect a refund for food that has been consumed, no matter how little weight was lost. Furthermore, some customers will simply be too embarrassed to admit their failure and ask for a refund. More importantly, for every customer who has their $20 fee returned, others will be so pleased with the initial results they will decide to lose 50 pounds. The extra 30 pounds are not at $1 per pound, and you still buy food from the center. This money-back guarantee is pure marketing genius.

- Be aware that guarantees sometimes carry negative marketing connotations that can reflect poorly on your image. That is largely due to all-too-common marketing promotions that border on deceptive advertising. I once had a client who previously developed a product marketed exclusively on late-night infomercials. You are no doubt familiar with the type of promotions to which I am referring. Everything is a huge value (whatever that is), yours for only $19.95 plus shipping and handling charges. The product always comes with a satisfaction guarantee. My client explained the rules of the game. The key phrase is "plus shipping and handling," a greatly inflated sum that includes the actual cost of the product. That explains why infomercials frequently offer a second item "free" if customers pay separate shipping and handling fees. The $19.95 is pure gross profit! If a disgruntled consumer wants a refund, they must first return the product at their expense. The shipping and handling is not refunded. Therefore, the seller's "worst-case scenario" is that the customer paid the full cost of the product and is now allowing them to resell it. Meanwhile, the refunded $19.95 was an interest free loan. I trust this deceptive practice is incompatible with your mission statement and value system. Again, do not risk long-term customer relations and reputation for the sake of short-term gains.

103. Customer uncertainty also includes the fear that you may simply not show up on time. We have all wasted hours or had plans ruined while waiting for a promised service call or delivery that never happened. Unquestionably, the best way to overcome this concern is through a solid reputation of dependable, on-time service. A quicker way may be to offer a guarantee. For example, there is a national franchise of HVAC contractors whose advertising slogan is "Always on time or you don't pay a dime."

- Aside from the cost of providing free service to already unhappy customers, this sort of guarantee may have other unintended consequences. Domino's Pizza was forced to discontinue its 30-minute guarantee in 1993 due to lawsuits arising from accidents allegedly caused by hurried delivery drivers.

I conclude the discussion of reducing risk to increase sales with a succinct quote by American author and motivational speaker Zig Ziglar. He said, "Statistics suggest that when customers complain, business owners and managers ought to get excited about it. The complaining customer represents a huge opportunity for more business."

Remind yourself of Mr. Ziglar's quote the next time you are forced to deal with an unhappy customer. Take it as an opportunity to learn more about their needs while reducing their perception of risk. Remember also that helping them address their needs and concerns is critical to the ultimate success of every business.

POTPOURRI FOR $200

Here is a thought provoking question for you. What exactly is potpourri? Aside from being a favorite Jeopardy category, can anyone actually tell me how and where the word is used? I suspect that like me, you have pondered those very questions many times.

Years of extensive research into the matter finally taught me that potpourri comes from the French words "pot" and "pourri." No surprises there. Pot has the same meaning as in English. Pourri means rotten. So literally, potpourri means a pot full of rotten stuff. Is it me, or do I suddenly sound like Gus Portokalos in *My Big Fat Greek Wedding*? Come to think of it, I much prefer baklava to Bundt cakes.

Well, as near as I can figure, in common usage potpourri is just a collection of mismatched stuff, some of it looking dried up and yes, perhaps even a little rotten. However, when you mix it all together, it actually looks and smells good. It has a purpose! In this chapter, I am going to present a potpourri of miscellaneous marketing ideas for you to consider in profitably growing your business. Just like potpourri, the results will look good on your bottom line.

Up Selling Existing Customers:

104. Earlier, I talked about the concept of "up selling" or second sales as Alan Zell called them. Up selling is not just for product sales. Many parents of adolescences will remember their first cell phone bill after a child discovered texting. I quickly learned that for only $4.99 a month, my oldest son could have had unlimited texting. When my youngest son started texting, I learned that unlimited texting for everyone on my plan was only $12.99. In both instances, I grudgingly paid one outrageous phone bill, only because switching carriers was not worth the effort. Your customers may not have that limitation. Assuming there are several levels of your services, take the initiative. Educate customers on the benefits of improved or expanded service levels before they learn the hard way, and decide to take their business elsewhere.

- Encourage prompt action and participation by offering customers an incentive to upgrade in the next 30 days.

105. It is easy to tell when my car needs gas. There is a gauge right on the dashboard. If I am not paying attention, a light comes on when the fuel level gets too low. Finally, the car will simply stop when the tank is completely empty. However, my car (unlike some models) gives no warning when I need an oil change. Even if your car displays remaining oil life, you must remember to scroll through the display to see it. Jiffy Lube, Kwik Kar and other oil change franchises have

solved that problem by putting a small transparent sticker on my windshield to remind me at what mileage I need an oil change. Doctors, dentists and veterinary clinics have long sent reminders when annual checkups are due.

Many consumer products that require periodic replacement or maintenance give no obvious warning. Filters on furnaces and air conditioners, and batteries in smoke detectors and watches all come to mind. Many things around the home and office including HVAC equipment, computers, alarms systems, pool equipment and so on all need periodic service for optimum efficiency. **If you sell replacement parts on products that fall into this category, or provide the actual service, create a diary system, a sticker or something to remind customers to schedule a service call.**

- Have the customer indicate how they want to be contacted for a reminder when they initially purchase the item or sign up for service. Provide several options such as email and phone calls. Both are cheaper and more likely to solicit a favorable response than mailing a card. Whatever diary system you choose, it is sure to improve customer retention.

- Create a sense of urgency by including a limited-time special offer with the reminder. A 10% discount, a free month of service or other incentive will discourage customers from procrastinating or purchasing services elsewhere.

- Everyone who subscribes to magazines has received next year's renewal notice within a few months of renewing the current year. In some cases, the marketing strategy may be to hope the subscriber forgot they still have 10 months remaining on their current subscription. However, in many cases the publisher offers substantial discounts to renew early, especially if pre-authorized to charge your credit card at renewal. The same idea applies to remind clients to renew annual contracts, maintenance agreements and so forth. Do not wait for the customer to contact you, and do not risk losing a sale simply because both you and the customer forgot. Again, offer customers a discount or an extra month on the contract if they renew by a specified date.

If you are a pet owner, you are aware of a powerful strategy veterinary clinics employ to drive sales and increase profits. That strategy is boarding facilities. Think about your experiences boarding pets. Chances are you also have them washed and groomed, and probably address checkups, shots and other recurring medical needs. Of the $65 average daily bill when boarding our Rottweiler, over half is for services other than boarding. I willing pay the $65 because it meets another important need. It buys the added assurance that if anything happens to my 11-year-old dog, she will be well taken care of until I return.

The point is that in addition to being profit centers in their own right, boarding facilities attract customers and generate revenue for other areas of veterinary clinics. Ask yourself, "What is an equivalent up selling strategy for my business?" To be successful, it needs to be complementary or counter-cyclical to your primary business. Here is an example of each strategy.

106. Starbucks announced a textbook example of a complementary marketing strategy in 2010. They began to test market beer and wine sales at several Seattle locations. Designed to supplement a product line that holds diminishing customer appeal after the morning rush hour, alcohol goes on sale at 4:00 PM. Starbucks also announced their Starbucks VIA® Ready Brew coffee in 2010. It comes in four flavors, and is available online and through grocery stores and other retail channels. Not surprisingly, it was widely reported in 2011 that Starbucks has replaced Burger King as the nation's third largest restaurant chain, a major accomplishment for a "non-burger and fries" chain.

107. Installing holiday lighting is big business in my town. Contractors spend most of November and early December installing lights. They spend January removing, repairing and storing lights for the summer. What do the installers do the rest of the year? I frequently see their trucks around town. I have also met several installers over the years. Everyone had a lawn maintenance or landscaping business that not coincidentally keep them busy from March through October.

More Event-based Marketing Ideas:

108. Small business coach and author Robert Gerrish said, "For many, one of the greatest moments in business is the joy of attracting a new customer or client. In such circumstances, it is easy to get so caught up in the excitement that we forget to spend time on realizing the value of one of our business's best assets, our existing client base." For example, you may have heard banks criticized for offering free checking to new customers while charging existing customers for the same service. As Mr. Gerrish suggests, too often promotions only target new prospects. Show your appreciation to existing customers by holding promotions and events designed exclusively for them.

- A special after-hours personal shopping event or trunk show, complete with entertainment, refreshments and "invitation only" discounts is an example. If your products typically require sizing or fitting (such as clothes), allowing a two day presale can create additional excitement. Customers select their purchases in advance, while you hold them until the actual sale. This procedure also requires customers to visit your facility at least twice.

- The luxury day spa I spoke of earlier invited my wife and I (did I mention she is one of their most loyal customers) to an art exhibit by a nationally recognized concert pianist. The event also included a wine tasting.

- A final caution about special event promotions is that in order to be truly special, you cannot hold them too often. **Any promotional tool that is used too frequently runs the risk of creating customer expectations that will cause them to avoid full price purchases in anticipation of a sale or event that may never happen.**

109. Another way to demonstrate your appreciation for existing customers, suppliers and employees is to hold an open house or reception. This is a great way to showcase your operations. It will also strengthen relationships between customers and staff that have not met. If your facilities do not include a suitable physical location, host it at your home, a nearby restaurant or under a tent on the front lawn. Moreover, while your open house or reception must be memorable, it does not have to be expensive. Class is not measured in dollars.

  - You may find network contacts are willing to help cater the event, print programs and menus, provide entertainment or other useful services at substantial discounts in order to promote their products and services to your customer base. Always take full advantage of your networks and be ready to reciprocate by supporting and promoting their events.

  - Avoid scheduling functions on weekends or when likely to conflict with numerous holiday events. Use all of the communications tools and options previously discussed to ensure good attendance. There is nothing more discouraging than hosting a party when no one shows up.

110. Why existing customers or new prospects visit your facility is usually not important. What is always important is simply that they visit. Attract attention by holding an event unrelated to your business. For example, if you are near a lake or river, hold a boat show. Have your town's luxury auto dealership conduct test drives in your parking lot soon after the new models come out. I previously mentioned the marketing power of car shows. An additional advantage is that the entry fee (typically $10 to $20) car owners expect to pay covers the cost of awards, making it a cost-free event for the host.

- **Select an event that is likely to excite and attract a wide audience, not just your existing customer base.**

- The first place to look for promotional ideas should be your networking groups.

- One school of thought says you should always charge for special events so customers assign a value to them. If you agree, tie this idea into Chapter 10 and promote the fact that all proceeds will be donated to a local charity. The charity will then become your marketing partner in ensuring the event is well attended.

Contests & Drawings:

111. Here is a suggestion so simple and inexpensive you may have overlooked it, even though you have seen it used hundreds of times. Put a bowl or attractive container next to your cash registers and invite departing customers and guests to drop their business card in for a chance to win a free meal, store gift card or something else of value. This suggestion can be very effective in adding names to your mailing list.

112. Contests can also be used to encourage customers to return to claim prizes. Create a sense of excitement. Promote them in your email campaigns, blogs, social media, etc. by announcing winners, next month's prizes, and so on. A slight variation of this simple marketing strategy is to select winners from customers who complete evaluation or survey forms.

    • Allow participants to post their contest entry on your Facebook Fan page. The catch is that to post on your wall, they must first "Like" your page.

    • Above all, conduct your contest with flair and elegance, or do not do it at all.

Endorsement Marketing:

113. Did you ever wonder why GMC is the "official truck" of the National Football League? It is not as if they haul injured players off the field on Sierra Hybrids. If they

did, can we assume the trucks would be using Castrol, the "official motor oil" of the NFL?

An even bigger question might be why Wingstop is the "official chicken wing" of the Dallas Cowboys. For that matter, do the Cowboys really need an official chicken wing and if so, do they taste better than unofficial wings? I am guessing the nutritional value is about the same. Wingstop is not wondering about those questions. Executive Vice President Andy Howard reported Sunday sales for the 2010 season were up 15 percent in spite of the Cowboys' disappointing 6 and 10 record.

Endorsement marketing is common in the insurance industry. For example, Hartford Insurance Company teamed up with the AARP to become the endorsed auto and home insurer to the AARP's reported 40 million members. The AARP also offers life insurance products through New York Life, and long-term care products through Genworth Financial Group.

I am not suggesting you attempt to negotiate a deal with the NFL or a million-member national organization. Start small, on a state or local level. Identify organizations whose members use your products or services. Associations are usually eager to earn income from sources other than their membership. For the cost of an associate membership, an advertisement in their quarterly newsletter or a booth at their annual convention, you can probably find trade associations and similar groups willing to designate your company as the official supplier for your product or service. That in turn provides access to their membership directory, and perhaps speaking engagements.

- A rule of thumb in the insurance industry is these marketing costs should not exceed two percent of anticipated revenue.

- The best place to find organizations is your state capital where many will be headquartered.

- If you are not prepared to market on a statewide basis, find out if there are local or regional chapters.

114. Do not overlook educational institutions and fraternal organizations as a source of endorsement sales. I knew a small business that was the preferred supplier of screen-printed and embroidered shirts for 50,000 students at Texas A&M University. How much is that endorsement worth? For the 2010 "Maroon Out" football game against Nebraska, one of many annual events the tradition-loving Aggies commemorate with shirts (I have paid for a closet full of them in recent years), the University's student body, alumni and supporters reportedly bought over 55,000 shirts. My unofficial source tells me the supplier was paid $3.50 apiece.

- Again, start small. You are more likely to land a profitable endorsement from a local high school sports team or a Parent-Teacher Association than from a major university. I also knew a one-shop sporting goods store that sold letter jackets for several large high schools. If you have raised a teenager in recent years, you know how expensive these customized items can be.

Free Delivery:

115. There is no such thing as a free lunch. The same can be said about free shipping. It is a variable cost of doing business. It ultimately must be passed on to customers, directly or through increased prices. So why did Wal-Mart, America's largest retailer, announce in early November 2010 that it was offering free shipping through December 20? Furthermore, why did competitors like Target and JCPenney quickly announce similar plans?

     The answer is they all read the same market research. Consumers love "free" shipping. It is as close to a guaranteed way of increasing customer satisfaction as you will find. Conversely, an online shopper survey by Compete.com reported that high shipping costs were the number-one reason online shoppers were not satisfied with their orders. It is also why 65% of respondents indicated they prefer the "in store pick up" option, when available.

     • If you decide to offer free shipping, test the bottom line impact by initially setting a minimum threshold (for example, only available on orders over $50) on sales. Accountability is a key to every successful marketing campaign, and this is no exception.

That completes my list of 115 Low-cost Ways to Avoid Market Obscurity. I end the list by reminding you of the first rule of marketing and customer relations.

Always under-promise and over-deliver.

In that spirit, and at no extra cost to the reader, I have included four additional marketing ideas. Like any self-respecting bean counter, I prefer to deal with numbers ending in zeros or fives. Writing a book called *119* Low-cost Ways to Avoid Market Obscurity would be wrong on so many levels. Here are your bonus marketing ideas.

116. Speaking of free delivery, here is an example of a business that found a creative way of using delivery as a marketing advantage without impacting their bottom line. A few years ago, one of the national pizza chains decided to offer a home delivered pizza that was larger than the in-store version. Customers willingly paid extra for the super-sized pizza, especially since it came with free delivery. They did not know (or did not care) that there was no incremental cost for the larger product. The extra price was in reality a hidden delivery charge. The moral of this example is simply that customer perceptions and opinions define value in every transaction. If they are reluctant or unwilling to pay for one service, perhaps they will perceive value in some other feature that can fund the cost of the first service.

117. Apartment complexes and storage facilities sometimes offer prospective new tenants a free month of rent. Health clubs offer a free month of membership services. What you may not have realized is the last month is the free one. The tenant or member must first sign a lease or contract, and then pay on time for twelve months. The same concept may work if you provide services that involve an on-going or recurring relationship. An example would be providing computer network support or monthly accounting services.

   • An added cash flow advantage exists if customers prepay the contract or commitment at the start of the term, or provide a security deposit.

118. Market intelligence can be defined as the collection, analysis and evaluation of information relevant to a company's financial outlook pertaining to its customers, products, industry and competition. The purpose of market intelligence is to make informed business decisions based on actual or anticipated developments, changes and trends. It is narrower in scope than a full-blown market research project, and therefore likely to be far cheaper in cost.

   For those of us who grew up during the Cold War watching James Bond, the phrase might sound very "MI6-ish," conjuring up images of high-tech surveillance gadgetry used by beautiful people as they race Aston Martins through the French Alps. In actual practice, market intelligence for the typical small businessperson is much more mundane and low tech. Nonetheless, the ability to monitor and anticipate market changes and competitor actions is a valuable tool for every business. It is sure to provide numerous opportunities for profitable growth.

Since it is low tech, it can also be low cost. We like low cost, right? City and regional business journals, the business section of local newspapers, the Internet, U.S. Census Bureau statistics, common customers and suppliers, commercial websites and even your eyes and ears are all potential sources of actionable information.

Governmental units and corporate America publish all sorts of relevant market data. The list is extensive. Governments disclose incorporations and new business formations, bankruptcy filings and business licenses. On property matters they publish real estate sales, mortgage financing activity, median home values, building permits, property foreclosures and zoning change requests and approvals. They also disclose bid requests and awards for public projects, marriages, divorces, sales tax revenue, public entity minutes and budgets, population and employment data. Businesses disclose new products, marketing campaigns, executive changes, new facility openings, interest rate changes, new customers and contracts.

What would it do for your marketing efforts if you could identify and capitalize on new sales opportunities before your competition does, or quickly counteract their promotions, price changes and other actions? For example, suppose you are one of several drywall contractors in your town. However, you are the first to learn that a large tract of undeveloped land was recently sold, and that a rezoning request to single-family residences is pending approval. While it could be weeks or even months before the new owners or general contractor requests formal bid proposals, you have already made your initial sales pitch.

You must identify information in the public domain relevant to your business. You can then decide what market actions are appropriate given your analysis. Look for one of two general types of information: direct actionable information such as recent or anticipated competitor actions; or, indications of trends and future developments.

- Begin identifying relevant information by answering several questions. The first question is who are your direct and indirect competitors? What actions might they take to make it easier or more difficult for you to compete with them? For example, if a competitor announces longer hours, a major sale or a new product line, your business life is about to get a little more challenging. On the other hand, if a national competitor announces the closure of their local facility, you may want to develop a marketing campaign to attract their former customers.

- Another question you should address is what factors are likely to increase or decrease your pool of potential customers. For example, most construction related businesses are significantly affected by interest rates; falling mortgage rates encourage home building, construction material sales and mortgage lending. Rising interest rates have the opposite effect. New car sales are impacted by the employment outlook; consumers are reluctant to incur additional debt if they fear the loss of their job. Conversely, car owners might then be expected to begin spending more on repairs as they are forced to maintain aging vehicles.

- Business and economic indicators can be leading or lagging. Leading indicators change at the start of a business cycle, and are therefore probably more important in your market intelligence. Mortgage rates in the previous bullet are a leading indicator of new home construction. As another example, assume your business is home decorating with a specialty in new construction. Additional leading indicators relevant to you may be building permits or new home starts in your city or region.

- Indicators can be directly or inversely correlated to your business. Sticking with the interest rate example, home construction is inversely related to mortgage rates. Again, construction rises as rates fall. One the other hand, if you own a job placement and staffing agency, your business is probably directly correlated to employment levels. Your placements increase as employers increase hiring activity. Another directly correlated (and in this case leading) indicator might be the level of help wanted ads.

I once had a boss who liked to say, "I get a lot of data. Very little information, but a lot of data!" Avoid the common mistake of confusing the two. Plan in advance of the data gathering process exactly what you expect to do with the information obtained. Collecting data without developing information and an action plan to capitalize on it is wasted effort.

119. Let me now end the complete list of cost effective marketing ideas by issuing a challenge. **Do something original, offbeat and maybe even a little crazy to grab customer attention and stand out from your competition.** Tasteful humor goes hand-in-hand with this suggestion. I know a consulting firm that adopted Groundhog Day as their official corporate holiday (they said all the good ones were taken) and Punxsutawney Phil as their company mascot. Every February 2nd, long after customers have thrown the last Christmas card away, they have received a card and gift from just one vendor for the last 15 years.

I heard about another small business that holds a pre-Christmas contest that invites customers to submit their favorite holiday recipe online. While modest prizes may be awarded for the best recipes, everyone is a winner. Every customer receives an electronic cookbook compiled from the entries, and just in time for their holiday meal planning.

- You might think about a themed promotion coinciding with something associated with your business, or a significant happening in your community. Above all, be original. A German restaurant holding an annual Oktoberfest celebration is logical, but it has been done many times before. On the other hand, did your team make it to the World Series, Super Bowl or the Stanley Cup? That is a rare occurrence worth celebrating.

- Not a sports person? Celebrate the Russian Ballet's arrival in town with an evening of dance lessons. Is a new Picasso exhibit opening at the art museum? Hold a contest for customers to paint their own version of *Guernica* and announce the winners and prizes at an art show.

- If no other ideas appeal to you, make up your own holiday and start a new marketing tradition that you can capitalize on for years to come. After all, if someone can designate March as National Adopt-a-Rescued-Guinea-Pig Month (I could not have made that one up), what is to stop you from using a little imagination?

The idea is simply to have fun communicating your brand, value proposition, products and services in a clever and original way that customers will remember. Let your creative juices flow! The only limitation is your own imagination in dreaming up a low-cost promotion.

I hope I have convinced you that having fun and communicating with your customers does not have to mean being able to afford a huge budget.

Chapter 13

LESSONS FROM COOL HAND LUKE

The 1967 movie *Cool Hand Luke* earned Paul Newman an Academy Award nomination for his portrayal of a nonconformist member of a southern chain gang. It also taught me two memorable lessons. The first is that some people can eat 50 eggs (you had to see the movie). Admittedly, that has never proven to be especially useful information. Nonetheless, it seems good to know. The second and more important lesson is that a failure to communicate can have potentially dire consequences.

As a CPA, I am tempted to explain away the reason for the high rate of business failures with the fact that they ran out of money. While undoubtedly a true statement, it is overly simplistic. It is also more descriptive of a symptom than the reason for the problem. **I believe the root cause of many failures is actually a failure to communicate with customers.** As you read and reflect on the list of marketing ideas, I think you will agree that the common thread throughout is communication. In fact, the word was used over 30 times in the previous pages.

Ultimately, communication is what successful marketing is all about. It is about establishing and strengthening customer relationships by communicating your message and your value statement to the right people, at the right time and using all the right channels. It is about that continual education and training process Robert Allen and Stuart Wilde stressed.

A review of some major milestones that have shaped business communications over the centuries will illustrate one final essential point. The point is this. Societies and consumers usually accept and embrace changes in communications faster than the business community can adapt to them. Even the most carefully designed marketing communiqué, be it a press release, an ad campaign, a newsletter, etc., is likely to fail if it is not transmitted in the optimal channel. The pace of change is escalating, thereby increasing the chances that businesses will fail to communicate their message to their customers and prospects.

As you review the timeline, think about how each change influenced the growth and success of businesses that were foresighted enough to embrace it. Consider also the wide variation in the useful lives of the various inventions, ranging from the printing press that has been around almost 600 years to the Pony Express that lasted less than two years. Lastly, imagine how businesses might have successfully adapted to further changes as each of the milestones were eventually displaced or relegated to a lesser importance by later means of communication.

Here are several examples of innovations that significantly influenced businesses:

A. Gutenberg's invention of the printing press in 1440 made the mass production of books possible. Mass production of newspapers followed in 1605. The first paid advertisements appeared in a French newspaper in 1836.

B. The United States Postal Service began in Philadelphia in 1775. Free mail delivery in U.S. cities began in 1863, reaching rural America by 1896.

C. On April 3, 1860, a single rider left St. Joseph, Missouri and headed west. He carried a pouch containing 49 letters and five telegrams. A rider carrying another pouch left San Francisco the same day and headed east. The Pony Express was born. Both pouches reached their destination ten days later. It was the fastest means of east-west communication in the days immediately preceding the Civil War. A 1/2 ounce letter cost $5 at the start of the service, or approximately $133 based on changes in the consumer price index through 2009.

D. Alexander Graham Bell was awarded a patent for the telephone in March 1876. The first "long distance" call between Cambridge and Boston, a distance of about three miles, occurred in October of that year. New York and Boston became the first cities linked by telephone in 1883.

E. George Eastman developed film technology to replace photographic plates in 1884. He founded Eastman Kodak in 1892. With the slogan "You press the button, we do the rest" he introduced photography to the masses with cardboard box cameras that sold for $1, the equivalent of $24 in 2009.

F. Chicago's R. H. Donnelley created the first Yellow Pages directory in 1886. The name was coined three years earlier when a Wyoming directory printer ran out of white paper and used yellow instead.

G. On November 2, 1920, Pittsburgh's KDKA reported the results of the national election that saw Warren G. Harding elected president of the United States. This was the first broadcast of a commercial radio station. Paid advertising followed within two years. Large companies like Westinghouse, Philco, Wrigley and Maxwell House Coffee typically sponsored entire programs.

H. Scottish inventor John Baird demonstrated the first television in London in 1925. The image had just enough resolution to discern a human face. Television was introduced to the public (including my father) at the 1939 New York World's Fair. Commercial television developed following World War II. Milton Berle became its first "superstar" in 1948. As with radio, broadcasts were usually sponsored by a single national advertiser including Texaco and Procter & Gamble. The first national broadcast of a show in color was NBC's Tournament of Roses Parade on New Year's Day 1954. Westinghouse began offering a color television in the New York City area about two months later. It sold for $1,295, or approximately $10,400 in 2009 inflation-adjusted dollars.

I. Two decades of research into communication networks, much of it related to government sponsored defense projects, culminated on August 6, 1991 when the European Organization for Nuclear Research introduced the World Wide Web. By 1994, there was a growing public interest. By June 2010, the estimated number of Internet users had reached two billion.

Now consider subsequent developments in business communication channels.

J. The days of printed books and newspapers may be numbered. Consider the following:

- Although Amazon keeps its sales figures close to its corporate vest, reports by Bloomberg and other sources suggests it likely sold over eight million Kindles in 2010. Amazon's January 27, 2011 press release reported, "Amazon.com is now selling more Kindle books than paperback books. Since the beginning of the year, for every 100 paperback books Amazon has sold, the Company has sold 115 Kindle books. Additionally, during this same time period the Company has sold three times as many Kindle books as hardcover books."

- Those sales were achieved in spite of stiff competition from the Apple iPad and other eReaders. Apple's January 2011 SEC filing said, "Net sales of iPad and related products and services were $4.6 billion and unit sales of iPad were 7.3 million during the first quarter of 2011. iPad was released in the U.S. in April 2010 and in various other countries over the remainder of 2010. As of December 25, 2010, Apple had distributed iPads in 46 countries."

- In an industry financed by advertisers, newspapers now cost more to reach a similar audience than radio, magazines, or websites. The Newspaper Association of America expected ad revenue to drop 9.7% in 2009 after falling 16.5% in 2008.

K. In a press release issued November 12, 2010, the U.S. Postal Service reported a loss of $8.5 billion in fiscal year 2010. They delivered 6.1 billion fewer pieces of mail than the previous year. Officially labeled advertising mail, 273 million pieces of daily junk mail make up 47% of Postal Service volume, but only 25% of its revenue.

L. Struggling from its failure to win a federal contract to deliver mail, the Pony Express announced its closure on October 26, 1861, two days after the transcontinental telegraph connected Omaha to Sacramento. During an 18-month existence, it succeeded in reducing the cost of a 1/2 ounce letter by 80%.

M. Home phones are being replaced by cell phones and other mobile devices. Smartphone users can now perform virtually any function available on a computer. They can also scan product bar codes for instant price comparisons and download directions to local competitors. In October 2010, CTIA-The Wireless

Association reported in their *50 Wireless Quick Facts* that over 89% of handsets operating on wireless networks are capable of browsing the web. They also quoted a 2010 Pew Internet survey that found 88% of teenage cell phone owners use text messaging.

N. With its market steadily evaporating since the 1975 invention of digital cameras, Kodak ended a 74-year run when it discontinued production of Kodachrome film in 2009. Their SEC filings reported a $210 million loss that year. The digital camera was invented by a Kodak engineer.

O. Borrell Associates, Inc. is a research and consulting firm that tracks local advertising. Their July 2008 report titled *Say Goodbye to Yellow Pages* estimated the industry would lose 39% of its revenue over the next five years as small businesses focus more on online advertising. It was forecasted that 2008 print revenue of $12.7 billion would decrease to $7.8 billion by 2013. In an age of instant information, an increasing number of businesses are obviously questioning the wisdom of spending scarce marketing resources on a medium that will not be distributed until months after incurring the expense. Some estimates suggest that up to 20% of small businesses do not survive to see their Yellow Pages ad in print. Meanwhile, concerns over the environmental impact of discarded books are causing cities to explore advanced recovery fee ordinances that will add millions of dollars to industry costs.

P. The marketing impact of satellite radio remains to be seen. Arbitron ratings show Sirius XM has 32 million weekly listeners in some highly desirable demographics. Yet, the publicly traded company reported a $343 million loss in 2009. Its stock has not traded above $2 a share in almost three years.

Q. A four-decade oligopoly by ABC, CBS and NBC began to crack by the 1980s. Having once controlled 99% of all broadcasts, their market share dropped to 32% by 2005 according to Douglas Blanks Hindman and Kenneth Wiegand of the *Journal of Broadcasting & Electronic Media*. The Fox Network now produces the highest rated show on TV (*American Idol*) and the longest running primetime show (*The Simpsons*). The increased popularity of cable TV, Internet access to programming and digital recording devices threaten to redefine television's role as the "high end" communications media. Fortunately, the ability to embrace technological changes has allowed television to hold the average American's attention for 4.7 hours a day (according to a 2008 Nielsen report) over 60 years after its introduction. Finally, NBC's owner Comcast announced in January 2011 that they were dropping the iconic peacock from their official corporate logo. This announcement ended a 56-year television tradition that first trumpeted the arrival of color programming to an entire generation of mesmerized children. Curse you, Comcast!

R. Lastly, the traditional model of text dominated static communications on a free World Wide Web navigated via a handful of search engines is being challenged. New paradigms including pay per click advertising, video and yes, social media are quickly redefining it.

As I reflect on this timeline, it occurs to me that very few people can anticipate, let alone shape communications in this accelerating stream of consumer driven changes. Names like Gates, Bezos, Zuckerberg and a handful of other young billionaires come to mind. The rest of us do well just to keep up with it.

Therefore, the goal of today's successful small businesses should be to meet customers in whatever communication channels they choose at that moment and to educate and influence (never dictate) consumer behavior as best they can.

I now end where I began. I remind you there is no "one-size-fits-all" magic formula for success; no one thing that will permanently solve your marketing challenges or slow the pace of change. What worked yesterday may not work tomorrow because as Tony Robbins and others have said, "The past does not equal the future!" That much is clear from the timeline. There is simply no substitute for hard work, vision and continuous planning and experimentation.

However, there is also much cause for hope. Earlier, I cited Don Bradley and Chris Cowdery's exhaustive study *Small Business: Causes of Bankruptcy*. This was their conclusion: "Evidence suggests that failure rates of small businesses in the United States are related to the nature of a capitalistic market in relying on competition where only the strongest survive. The causes for small business failure and ultimately bankruptcy are many. A successful entrepreneur is, no doubt, the consummate businessperson who must be a jack-of-all-trades. **It is evident that nearly all entrepreneurs have the opportunity to control their own destiny. Success is obviously not a guarantee, but nor is failure.** A well-rounded businessperson who has carefully planned and prepared with a clear vision of who and what the company is will have an excellent opportunity for success."

I also point out that many of the marketing ideas discussed in this book would not have been possible just a few short years ago. Many more have been made easier and more cost efficient by recent technological developments and increased Internet-based competition.

I therefore challenge and encourage you to seize the opportunity to control your own destiny, to embrace change, to experiment with new ideas, and to learn from your triumphs and your disappointments in these exciting times. Your business will grow in the process.

I wish you great success in your efforts and I hope you have fun in your journey.

Appendix I

COMPETITION IS ALL ABOUT ME

DEFINING YOUR BASIS OF COMPETITION

As a parent, I tried to instill in my sons an awareness that the world did not revolve around them. Always think of others, be generous and sharing, and so on, often foreign concepts to a child.

As a father of college students, I preached less charitable concepts. The unfettered application of the same Robert Fulghum-ish principles that taught them to share their toys and wait their turn in line foretells disaster in a world where over 80% of businesses fail before their fifth anniversary.

We live in an Internet crazed universe where potential customers are only a few clicks away from a myriad of rival goods and services. Our zero-sum business world demands you think of yourself. Why for example would a customer rather deal with you than someone across town or even across the globe? This harsh reality can be summarized in one word: competition!

There is nothing original about the suggestion that competition is by its very nature selfish. Adam Smith explained his concept of the "invisible hand" in *The Wealth of Nations* in 1776. He said, "It is not from the benevolence of the butcher, the brewer, or the baker that we expect our dinner, but from their regard to their own self-interest. We address ourselves, not to their humanity but to their self-love, and never talk to them of our own necessities but of their advantages."

The same observation can be made of consumer behavior. Of all the reasons customers may choose to buy from you instead of your competition, self-interest is far more likely to be a motivating factor than a sense of benevolence.

Today's vernacular is "what's your value proposition." In *Creating and Delivering Your Value Proposition: Managing Customer Experience for Profit* authors Barnes, Blake and Pinder offer this definition, "A value proposition is an analysis and quantified review of the benefits, costs and value that an organization can deliver to customers and other constituent groups within and outside of the organization."

Simply stated, what is it you do better, faster, cheaper, etc. than your competition? In other words, how do you differentiate yourself in the market place? Author and market positioning expert Jack Trout summed up his view of the paramount importance of this matter in his book, *Differentiate or Die: Survival in Our Era of Killer Competition.* How you define, manage and exploit those advantages at a profit is the most fundamental strategic decision facing every entrepreneur.

Businesses define their value proposition within the context of three attributes. They are product, service and price, as illustrated in the following simple diagram.

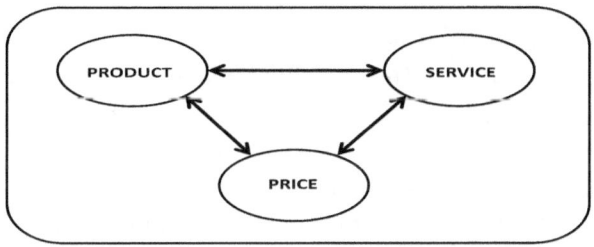

These attributes are multi-faceted and occasionally overlapping. A business can actually compete on any two. However, as shown in the diagram, never on all three. It is simply not possible in the long run to profitably offer the best products, supported by the highest level of service at the lowest price.

Product competition can involve offering the highest quality, the widest selection, or both. The Neiman Marcus catalog includes 15 men's designer watch manufacturers, including Cartier and Gucci. Timex watches may keep on ticking, but they will not be ticking at Neimans any time soon. Quality can be inherent in the product, or exist largely as a perception of the buyer. Car manufacturers have known and exploited this for years. Is a Lexus really worth $10,000 more than a comparably equipped Toyota? To the image conscious consumer, the answer is obviously yes.

Service can take many forms and be at point-of-sale, after the sale or both. As previously mentioned, L.L.Bean was ranked highest in customer service by *Business Week* in 2008. The Company pioneered the "lifetime satisfaction guarantee" almost 100 years ago. Visitors to Freeport, Maine are regaled with stories like the fisherman who stopped by at 2:00 A.M. (being open 24 hours is also an important aspect of their value proposition) to return boots purchased years earlier, no questions asked!

Contrast that to the experience of trying to find a sales assistant at the typical "big box" store. Competitive service advantages can encompass product ordering facilities, purchase terms, gift wrapping, comfortable waiting rooms, free Wi-Fi, delivery and even a friendly smile. Features such as free shipping, financing and money-back guarantees can blur the line between service and price.

A textbook example of a business that competes on price is Sam's Club. In the past five years, I have spent 50% more at Sam's than a high-end grocery store two blocks from my house. I have purchased groceries, printers, digital cameras, gasoline, office supplies, toiletries, pet food, bedding, toys, books, clothes and car tires. One day a guy actually talked me into whitening my teeth.

Why do I prefer Sam's to the closer store? The former operates as a giant warehouse bereft of employees and shopping bags, while the latter walks half-full grocery bags to my car as I sip lattes from their espresso bar. I buy undifferentiated products not requiring service from an array of acceptable if ever changing manufacturers, but always at Sam's consistently low prices. I find value in that assurance. I can also make my own lattes.

A final caution is in order for those businesses relying on pricing as their primary strategy. It is getting harder to make a buck in your increasingly crowded world.

Watch TV commercials and ask yourself which of the three types of competition is promoted most often. In a stagnant economy with 15 million people unemployed, it is tempting to lure customers solely with low prices. They are objective and quantifiable. Product and service are more subjective and far less reliable a basis on which to make rational consumer decisions.

A key marketing challenge is that if someone patronizes a business only because of low prices, they tend not to develop customer loyalty. Another challenge is the ease with which competitors can match lower prices. Many retailers are capitalizing on the tendency to compete on price by providing in-store comparisons, often matching the lowest advertised price. In an age of instant information (or "friction free capitalism" as Bill Gates called it) where any consumer with a smartphone can check competitors' prices on the spot, there is no reason to assume this trend will do anything other than accelerate, or that consumer behavior will change.

After all, when I was teaching my sons to share, I would have gently corrected them with a not-so-invisible hand if I caught them sharing Daddy's hard-earned cash with corporate America.

Did I get it right, Mr. Smith?

ABOUT THE AUTHOR

Dale R. Schmeltzle, CPA is the Managing Partner of CFO America, LLC, professional consultants dedicated to helping small business owners define, implement and monitor the tactical and strategic elements necessary to achieve long-term operational and financial success. CFO America provides fractional or part-time CFO and executive management expertise not available on an in-house basis.

Dale graduated summa cum laude from Bloomsburg University with a Bachelor of Science in Accounting, and has done graduate studies in finance at Temple University. His 35-year career as a consultant and employee includes senior financial management and operating responsibilities in a variety of service, accounting, financial and non-profit companies ranging from major divisions of Fortune 500 companies to startups. These assignments have spanned a continuum from publicly traded entities with thousands of employees to family businesses operating through virtual employees. They include workout situations and leveraged buy-outs.

Mr. Schmeltzle has been involved in raising over $1 billion of capital through initial and secondary public offerings, private placements, venture capital funding and bank debt. He was the Treasurer & Controller of the first successful leveraged buy-out in his industry's history.

Dale has been a frequent author and speaker for numerous professional associations and non-profit groups on a wide variety of subjects. He has taught college level finance and accounting courses to non-business audiences. He contributes his time and talents to community and business causes including having served on the board of a non-profit school, a volunteer management consultant at a nursing home, vice president of a national trade association, a member of a church finance committee and finance chairman of a national risk management organization.

Please visit www.cfoamerica.biz and www.CFOAmerica.net for more information. You can also follow CFO America on Facebook at www.facebook.com/CFOAmerica and on Twitter at http://twitter.com/#!/CFOAmerica.

www.ingramcontent.com/pod-product-compliance
Lightning Source LLC
Chambersburg PA
CBHW051515170526
45165CB00002B/481